CHAMPIONS

CHAMPIONS

MICHAEL MAGEE *with photographs by* PAT BAYES

William Morrow and Company, Inc.
New York

**Library of Congress
Catalog Card Number 80-82421**

ISBN   0-688-03716-X

© DESIGN BY Frank Newfeld

PRINTED AND BOUND
IN CANADA
BY BRYANT PRESS
FIRST U.S. EDITION

1   2   3   4   5   6   7   8   9   10

Contents

Acknowledgements

We would like to thank the following for their kindness, patience and invaluable assistance:

Ian Balding, Michael Bramwell, Ed Bowen, Greg Cable, Willie Carson, Fred C. Dobbs, Jane Goldstein, Mo Hall, Major W. Hern, Gus Koch, The Lynch-Bell's, The McCain Family, Peter Poole, Dianne Richardson, Dave Stevenson, W.K. Taylor, Joe Thomas, Bruce Walker, Peter Walwyn, Li and Dennis Weinrich, Charles Whittingham, and Maurice Zilber;

Bluegrass Farm, Claiborne Farm, Gainesway Farm, Highclere Stud, The National Stud (Newmarket), Spendthrift Farm, Walmac Farm, Windfields Farm (Oshawa and Chesapeake City), The John Ward Training Centre, The Ontario Jockey Club, The Daily Racing Form, The North American Bloodstock Agency, *and a good many others*.

MICHAEL MAGEE

PAT BAYES

Toronto, 1980

For
thoroughbreds
everywhere,

and those who devote
their lives to them.

Foreword

When Michael Magee first discussed the idea for this book with me I was curious as to what it would be called. When he told me *Champions*, I felt that it was a good title and a much better one than *The Champions* which would run the risk of offending someone. After all, it is always easier in any given decade to discuss the relative merits of racing's champions than to find a consensus on who they are. But it is this kind of discussion as to just who might be the best that keeps so many of us fascinated with the sport.

Now Michael Magee is as enthusiastic about racing and its future as anyone I've ever known. It would be fair to say that he is having a life-long love affair with the sport. So it pleases me to contribute the foreword to his book because along with him and many others I share in the sense of awe and wonderment at racing's achievements in the seventies. When saying this, I mean the achievements of the stars of the show, the horses themselves.

The appearance of so many champions in the last decade raises a number of questions. The most obvious one and the most difficult to answer is, "Why so many?" I believe it was because better horses were bred to better horses. And more than anything else, I think it was the new international aspect of racing that made these champions possible. The bloodstock that breeders in North America acquired from Europe years ago paid off.

The experience with our operation at Windfields in Oshawa, Ontario and Maryland illustrates the point. We imported the great *Nearco* line to Canada through *Nearctic*. *Nearctic* sired *Northern Dancer*, *Northern Dancer* sired *Nijinsky II* and *The Minstrel*, and with the accomplishments of these two the bloodstock we imported eventually went full-circle.

We now have a world-wide market for our breeding stock, because *Northern Dancer* made Windfields an international name in racing. His influence is as great in North America as it is in Europe. What perhaps impressed so many people about him was that he was a different type. He was not the standard, conventional classic horse, but a neater, more compact, stronger kind of horse with tremendous speed and acceleration. *The Minstrel* is very much like him; he, too, puts his stamp on his foals. *Nijinsky II* doesn't do quite as well with his two-year olds, but his three-year-olds and older horses are well worth waiting for. They are of the highest class in both North America and Europe. In fact, *Nijinsky II* might just outdo the 'Old Man.'

In the sixties and seventies, we at Windfields, along with other North American breeders, raised horses that excited buyers in Europe. We started to export. And in the thoroughbred market in the seventies, if North American buyers were off, foreign buyers were on. The Europeans followed the Japanese to our big North American sales. Certain currency restrictions eventually proved harmful to the Japanese, but British buyers filled the gap, especially with the pound going up and the dollar going down. Now Arab buyers are contributing greatly to the stabilization of the thoroughbred market. To my mind, this transoceanic movement of the best bloodstock goes a long way towards explaining the appearance of so many champions.

This movement was aided by other factors, such as improved air transportation for horses, for example; they are now jet travellers. Also of great importance, I think, was the computerization of information and records and the easy access to them through first-class communications systems. We now know what we're all doing because we're all much more interested and willing to exchange information. Ten years ago it was often difficult to find out what was going on elsewhere.

Another factor contributing to better breeding, to some extent, is the tremendous demand at the top of the market. It is probably correct to say that the cost of the average thoroughbred is not too inflated by today's standards, but the cost of the 'star attraction' yearling, the international one, is very high indeed. Some people are investing in horses as a hedge against inflation, just as they would invest in precious metals or gems. For others, record yearlings are conversation pieces. People like to say they own a son or daughter of *Secretariat*.

It is an indication of how racing has changed that nowadays everyone knows what that means. Ten years ago people outside the racing business wouldn't have appreciated a reference to a son or daughter of *Hyperion*. There's no doubt that television is responsible for this. Ever since *Native Dancer*, back in the days of black and white television, became the first thoroughbred to attain mass celebrity appeal, racehorses have made good TV stars. Everyone can see them and have an opinion.

Another change in North American racing that served to increase the number of champions is the popularity of turf racing. When the Washington, D.C. International was inaugurated more than twenty-five years ago, turf racing was a novelty. Now if a horse fails on the conventional dirt track there is always the chance of success on the turf. (Very few horses ever seem to excel equally on both.) Many horses that otherwise would have been unknown have found a home on the turf. And horses stay sounder and race longer on grass than they do on dirt. We must have dirt racing because our racing seasons are so long, but there's no denying that dirt racing is harder on our horses.

Nearly all of our turf courses are very small by European standards, resulting in more crowding, so luck plays a much bigger part on our small infield oval turf courses. If you run a mile and a half race on the dirt on a mile and a half track or even a mile track, the best horse on the day will usually win. When you card the same race on a seven-eighths of a mile turf track, the best horse on the day may not always win. What is good about the turf race is that nearly everyone will take a chance and run so you will usually have a race that will fill. The same race on the dirt probably would not. This unpredictability has helped turf racing to be taken very seriously in North America. Best of all it gives the racegoing public much better variety during a day at the races, and so contributes to the increased popularity that is so important to the future of racing.

That future will be better served when all the people involved can broaden racing's base. I'm afraid that I'm a one-thought man on this subject. I believe the way to broaden the base in North America is clearly off-track betting along the lines of the system in Australia. The Australian track operators handle both on-track and off-track betting, and the entire horseracing industry shares in the benefits. If we don't expand racing's base through off-track betting, then racing is going to deteriorate and breeding is going to deteriorate. Off-track betting is the key, I think, to what we have to have over the next few years. Also needed is the improvement of our racecourses and their facilities, but this cannot be done until the market for racing has been expanded.

If we want to go on raising and racing champions like those profiled in this book, then we will all have to work harder to ensure a stronger and healthier sport. I have no doubt that this can be accomplished. I can only hope that it will.

E.P. TAYLOR

Oshawa, Canada
1980

Affirmed

Affirmed captured the last American Triple Crown of the decade in a heroic struggle.

Alleged

His triumphant victories in The Prix de l'Arc de Triomphe marked *Alleged* as a great champion.

Allez France

She was tough and tenacious and for a time *Allez France* reigned supreme in European racing.

Dahlia

Dahlia garnered the rich prizes of two continents before retiring to Kentucky's Bluegrass Farm.

Exceller

Tremendous intelligence and courage is etched upon the face of *Exceller* who gave all he had.

Affirmed

The vast Spendthrift Farm stallion
paddocks in Lexington, Kentucky
contain some of racing's foremost
sires. The great *Native Dancer*
line has unrivalled representation
with three generations.

Affirmed, the youngest, now shares
a fence with his sire *Exclusive
Native*, who seems bemused by his son's
youthful boisterousness. In the
stable not far away is *Exclusive
Native's* sire *Raise a Native*.

Records are made to be broken, so
it is certain that with increasing
racing purses *Affirmed*'s world-
record earnings will be surpassed,
perhaps early in the eighties.
It will be difficult, however, to
upstage his great achievements.

15

Affirmed

Like *Secretariat, Seattle Slew* and
Spectacular Bid, Affirmed was very
much a North American television
star. His monumental struggles with
Alydar excited millions of viewers.

He will always be remembered, not
just for the money he won, but for
the way he won it. An unforgettable
champion, he always struggled to win.

Alleged

After *Alleged*'s second win of Europe's richest
race, the Prix de l'Arc de Triomphe, he was
retired to stud at Walmac Farm in Lexington.
Even after the rigors of the mandatory
quarantine period, he arrived at the farm
looking as compact and classy as he had on the
turf. Of all the champions of the seventies,
Alleged came closest to a perfect record –
nine wins in ten starts.

The
Queen
of
Longchamp

Allez France triumphed over her peers in her brilliant European racing career and overcame many formidable obstacles as a broodmare at Spendthrift Farm in Lexington.

During her first year in residence at the farm she was bred to Triple Crown winner *Secretariat* and sadly delivered a dead foal. After a year's rest, she was bred to *Northern Dancer* and came up barren. A subsequent mating with *Seattle Slew* resulted in the birth of a beautiful, healthy little filly.

Allez France

Although she is only three weeks old in these photographs, *Allez France*'s little filly already shows signs of her breeding. She delights in racing around her paddock and is remarkably inquisitive and brave about visitors.

Dahlia

*"She could
run
all day"*

It took a special
kind of toughness
for this great
mare to triumph on
both sides of the
Atlantic during her
long and gruelling
racing seasons.
Her victories were
resounding.

Around the racetrack
she was always
very determined to
do things her way, yet
she endeared herself
to those who worked
with her. She has
mellowed on the farm.
Motherhood definitely
agrees with her.

A broodmare's life
is fully programmed.
The average pregnancy
lasts 340 days, after
which she will nurse
the foal for roughly
13 weeks. Then it
will be weaned from
her side. During this
time she will probably
be bred to another
stallion until she
comes into foal again.
The cycle is repeated,
barring any complications,
until she is no longer
able to bear.

Dahlia

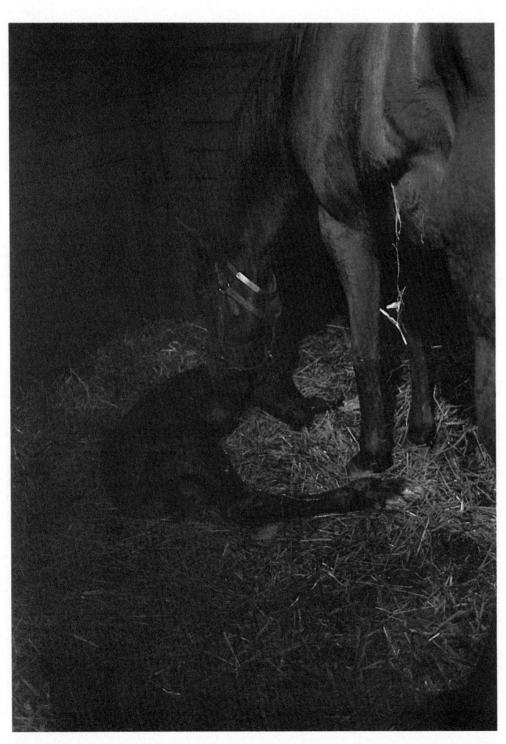

Dahlia was retired to Bluegrass Farm in Lexington. Bred to *Bold Forbes* she delivered a fine colt. Now named *Indomitable*, he is training in France under Maurice Zilber, who feels very encouraged by his progress. She then was bred to *What A Pleasure* and gave birth to another colt. He is being broken-in as a yearling on the farm. European champion *J.O. Tobin* is the sire of *Dahlia's* first foal of the eighties.

Dahlia has had relatively trouble-free pregnancies and deliveries. The *J.O. Tobin* foal was no exception. He arrived one day ahead of schedule. Within minutes of her waters breaking, *Dahlia* had given birth to the beautiful little colt. Four minutes later she was on her feet, and lovingly began to wash her new son. He was a bay, and as the shock of his new surroundings began to wear off, he struggled to get to his feet. On incredibly wobbly legs, after twenty minutes, he finally managed to stumble about the stall. Shortly after, he began to nurse. It may be a commonplace occurrence, but it always seems miraculous.

Twelve hours later, *Dahlia* and son are turned out into their paddock, for it is vital that the foal's legs drain of any fluid and the hooves harden.

Exceller

Trainer Charles Whittingham despaired when he met *Exceller* after the horse had arrived from his European campaign. "When he first walked off the van, I said three Hail-Mary's." *Exceller* walked stiffly, a bad sign, and seemed to be the worse for wear. But the trainer's misgivings proved unfounded.

Exceller

Exceller reluctantly adapted to his new surroundings, and devoted himself to the business at hand. During his American career he provided racegoers with some of the most exciting finishes of the decade. He raced with tremendous heart, and even gamely finished third in his last race despite suffering an injury in the running. "He was never a horse that you could get close to," according to those who worked around him. Perhaps this was due to how seriously he took his racing.

Happily, at Gainesway Farm in Lexington *Exceller* now seems to be able to relax in a way that he simply never could before. He shares a small barn with his great sire *Vaguely Noble* and his former racing and stable companion *Youth*. He goes about his stallion duties with the same enthusiasm that he showed on the racetrack. Expectations for his future at stud are high.

Affirmed

The Belmont Stakes at New York's Belmont Park has a greatness about it that few of the Classics can match. Its conditions call for three-year-old colts and geldings to carry 126 pounds, fillies 121 pounds, over a distance of a mile and a half. Few people would claim that the Belmont has the fame or the glamour of the Kentucky Derby, but most would agree that as a Classic race the Belmont is the true test of a champion.

In the 1978 Belmont Stakes, two champions were tested, not one. And probably no two horses in the long and distinguished history of New York racing came through in such incredibly gallant fashion as *Affirmed* and *Alydar*. It was their ninth meeting, with the score so far *Affirmed* six wins, *Alydar* two. They had raced one another for about eight miles and at the finish only three short lengths were between them.

Everyone at Belmont on that beautiful June day seemed to sense that this Belmont Stakes was going to be a struggle of historic significance. The two main rivals looked the part as they entered the walking-ring. Their readiness was more than obvious as they stood patiently during their saddling. Then, as they were walked slowly around, the vast crowd of people both inside and outside the ring kept comparing them. *Affirmed* was the lighter chestnut, lighter in colour, lighter in size, handsome in his own way, alert, controlled. *Alydar*, the better looking one, had more size and a richer colour of chestnut, but was now stained with sweat from knowing it would soon be time to run.

The drama was heightened by the arrival of the jockeys. For the winner in a few short minutes there would be a moment in racing he would never forget. Thousands watched young Steve Cauthen, the Kentuckian who had been racing's overnight sensation the season before. He looked almost too young to be relied upon in such a situation. He seemed somehow marked in his splendid flamingo, black and white, the colours of the powerful breeding and racing operation of Harbor View Farm owned by Louis and Patrice Wolfson, colours that the Wolfsons' trainer Laz Barrera had come to be associated with. Of equal interest to the crowd was the *Alydar* team. Jockey Jorge Velasquez looked terribly professional just standing there in the devil's red and blue of the world-famous Calumet Farm. Admiral and Mrs. Gene Markey and trainer John Veitch all had great confidence in him.

Alydar had been getting closer. At Churchill Downs in the Derby, he had finished second to *Affirmed* by a length and a half. In Baltimore, at Pimlico in the Preakness, he had still lost, but only by a neck. Now came the Belmont, the longest one of all. Only five horses made up the field. *Affirmed* was the favourite at 3–5, *Alydar* was a strong second choice at 11–10, then came *Darby Creek Road* at 10, *Judge Advocate* at 30 and *Noon Time Spender* at 38.

The track bugler finally called the field to the post and the vast throngs in the stands sent up an incredible cheer. *Darby Creek Road* with Angel Cordero Jr. up was the first horse to emerge from the tunnel connecting the walking-ring with the racetrack itself. By now everyone was standing. Then, there they were, the challenger *Alydar* and Velasquez. A huge roar went up to herald their arrival. *Alydar* was very much on edge. The third horse to appear caused an even greater uproar. *Affirmed* and Cauthen calmly, but decisively emerged. They had the burden. It was now or never to become the eleventh horse in the history of American racing to win the Triple Crown.

As the field paraded past the stands, the band played

"The Sidewalks of New York". Everyone remained standing, wanting to see absolutely everything that was going to happen. Now it was time for the starting gate to be placed across the track just before the finish wire directly in front of the packed stands. The anticipation of the crowd was beginning to be unbearable as the small field approached the gate. There was a tremendous nervousness as the field loaded, then a shock as *Judge Advocate* lunged through his stall in a rebellious manner. He was quickly loaded again and for a short space of time the gate held them all. It was only a second or two, but it was long enough to underline the start of one of the greatest races ever seen.

Affirmed broke on top. He was in the middle, with two horses on either side. Cauthen had him rolling and thousands were shouting, "C'mon Steve". *Judge Advocate* was second on the outside. *Alydar* passed up a chance to be on the inside as Velasquez decided to go after his rival on the outside. When they reached the backstretch *Affirmed* was still in front and still out from the rail. *Alydar* was ranging up on his outside. At the half-way point, the three-quarter pole, it was still *Affirmed* leading by a half a length, with *Alydar* second. From there to the mile there was no change in the order. On the huge turn for home *Affirmed* continued in front, but *Alydar* was now right with him. The race had turned into a speed duel, the race everyone had expected.

At the quarter pole, a quarter of a mile now from the finish, *Affirmed* led by the narrowest of margins. They turned for home. Into the stretch the two were still there, right together, side by side, stride for stride. *Alydar* was now so close that Cauthen barely had room to continue urging *Affirmed* on. Suddenly they were at the black and white eighth pole and Cauthen hit *Affirmed* one more time right-handed, then switched his whip to his left hand. For twelve more seconds that seemed totally desperate Cauthen managed to hit *Affirmed* twelve more times. *Affirmed* somehow, some way, held on; he did not give way, but neither did *Alydar*. Then, there it was– *Affirmed* with his head, and no more than his head, coming in the final crucial yards to desperately win one of the toughest stretch duels ever seen. Cauthen rose up and waved his whip in a confirming victory salute.

The tumult that followed took what seemed like ages to die down. The feeling seemed one of great relief that what the crowd had just seen had really happened. *Affirmed*, such a likeable horse, had managed to do it, and to do it the hard way. No American Triple Crown winner had ever had to work the way he did.

The win by a head after a gruelling mile and a half will never be forgotten, but *Affirmed* will be remembered for many other reasons. They say good ones win first out, and *Affirmed* did that at 14–1. At two he didn't look the part; he was too small, but he could run. He was the best two-year-old colt or gelding in America and developed into one of the toughest prospects for the three-year-old Classics in many years. At two he raced nine times and won seven. He won from five and a half furlongs to a mile and a sixteenth. He won in the east, the west, and the east again. Fortunately, he could be flown from one coast to the other with no bad results.

His wins took him to the winner's circles of Belmont, Saratoga and Laurel, as well as Hollywood Park. His liking for Hollywood was obvious. In three seasons he never lost at the Inglewood track. In fact, he came to know the track so well that one morning he ran off by himself. After a frantic search his handlers found him safe in his stall which he had somehow managed to find by himself–no mean feat in a stable area with 2,244 stalls.

He was blessed with the best of people too. His owner-breeders, the Louis Wolfsons, had that all important confidence so necessary for the proper management of a top horse. Their confidence was in their knowledge that their trainer Laz Barrera was the finest, and therefore knew what was best for *Affirmed*. Barrera's decisions for training were crucial and were continually proved correct. And he engaged Angel Cordero, Laffit Pincay Jr. and, most of all, Steve Cauthen to do the riding. These choices were always wise.

As a three-year-old, *Affirmed* spent the early months of 1978 training and racing in Los Angeles, often in bad weather. At Santa Anita he started three times and won them all, including the rich Santa Anita Derby. Two weeks later he won the even richer Hollywood Derby at Hollywood Park, and from there he picked up the three jewels of the Triple Crown, each time with a fight that must have left its mark.

Affirmed was not the favourite going into the Triple Crown series, particularly among the Blue Grass State locals. Old Kentucky hardboots tend to favour their own, especially at Derby time, and *Alydar* was the perfect horse for them. A son of *Raise A Native*, *Alydar* had been bred in the state by the legendary Calumet Farm, a force so powerful in its heyday that no stable could match its record in 'The Run for the Roses'. *Whirlaway, Pensive, Citation, Ponder, Iron Liege, Tim Tam* and *Forward Pass* had all won the Derby's first prize for Calumet, and *Alydar*, undefeated in the winter, was expected to carry on the tradition by repeating his victorious Flamingo, Florida Derby and Blue Grass stretch-runs. His winter Classics had been fast, only a tick or two off the course records at Hialeah and Gulfstream.

In the nine days between the Blue Grass at Keeneland and the Derby at Churchill Downs, *Alydar*'s morning drills were deliberately slow. John Veitch did not want him to be over-trained. A week before the Derby Laz Barrera did just the opposite with *Affirmed*, working him one mile and an eighth in 1:56-1/5 on an off-track at Churchill Downs, a work that was faster than *Affirmed*'s California Derbies for the distance. On the Wednesday of Derby week *Affirmed* went five furlongs in :59 flat, proving that he was now as fit as human hands could make him.

The first Saturday in May was a day of great anticipation. The weather was clear and the track was fast. The vast crowd made *Alydar* the 6–5 favourite; *Affirmed* was 9–5. Eleven horses sprang from the gate, triggering a huge roar from the stands and infield alike as *Raymond Earl* opened up a two-length lead. He was soon displaced by *Sensitive Prince* in a fast half of :45-3/5, almost two seconds faster than *Secretariat*'s :47-2/5 in 1973 when he broke the Derby record. Steve Cauthen, in his first Derby ride and in his home state, kept *Affirmed* in reserve four lengths back. Far back in ninth position was *Alydar* with Jorge Velasquez. The *Alydar* supporters were confident that he would benefit from the sizzling early pace.

After the three-quarter-mile mark, with half a mile to go, Cauthen asked *Affirmed*. On the second turn the answer was swift and decisive as the Harbor View Farm runner boldly took the lead. Into the stretch Cauthen rode like a veteran when briefly headed by *Believe It* and Eddie Maple. *Affirmed* came back and responded to strong urging to win by a length and a half. *Alydar* was second after a sluggish beginning not made any easier by some late bumping with the third-place finisher *Believe It*. The hardboots were impressed by *Affirmed*'s race, but they thought the Florida-bred might be tested more in the Preakness.

Two weeks later the *Affirmed-Alydar* road show was on again at old Pimlico. *Affirmed* and Cauthen were away well and moved past the front-runner *Track Reward* leaving the first turn. Down the backstretch it was *Affirmed* in front, with *Alydar* and Velasquez beginning to take much closer order. Cauthen rated *Affirmed* to perfection so that when *Alydar* and Velasquez reached him he still had more to go on. Into the stretch they raced together. *Affirmed* was on the inside, *Alydar* was on the far-outside. Velasquez was asking *Alydar* to challenge for all he was worth, and the response was a thriller, especially for the *Alydar* supporters. Their stretch-runner was at long last right beside his speedy nemesis and the entire stretch-run was still to

come. But *Affirmed* and Cauthen held fast, then improved their position in the race to the wire. At the finish *Affirmed* was the winner by a neck. *Alydar* was second again, seven and a half lengths ahead of *Believe It*.

Three weeks later *Affirmed* proved in the Belmont that if ever there was something he would respond to it was being looked in the eye, especially by *Alydar*.

He followed the taking of the Triple Crown with a win in Saratoga's Jim Dandy Stakes. Old racing men say that Saratoga is the graveyard of favourites and *Affirmed* at 1–20 almost proved them right, but he made it. Then, with Laffit Pincay Jr. in the saddle, he won the historic Travers, but his number came down for causing interference. The horse he had interfered with was *Alydar* in this, the tenth and final time they would meet. In the Marlboro Cup at Belmont, *Affirmed* was no match for the four-year-old *Seattle Slew*, and this loss was followed by a disastrous fifth-place finish at the same track when his saddle slipped in the Jockey Club Gold Cup. He was still judged champion three-year-old colt or gelding and Horse of the Year for 1978, however. His Triple Crown was too bright to ignore.

In 1979 at four, *Affirmed* began badly, losing his first two starts at Santa Anita's great winter meet. There were two problems. Now that he was maturing, he needed more time to train, time that was simply not there. Secondly, his regular jockey Steve Cauthen was in an unprecedented slump. Laz Barrera then made one of the most difficult decisions in his life. He replaced Cauthen with Pincay.

Though often battling to keep his weight down to an 'employment level' of 117 pounds, a battle waged with a diet of twelve unsalted peanuts mixed with bran for breakfast, a similar feast in the evening and, for afternoon strength, a lunch of boiled egg and crackers, Pincay was a perennial leader on the west coast whose mounts had earned over $50,000,000. Four times in the seventies he was champion American jockey. If anyone could get *Affirmed* out of the doldrums, it had to be Pincay.

A smashing ten-length win at a mile and a quarter in the Charles H. Strub Stakes in February showed that *Affirmed* was back in form again. Then at the finish of the mile and a quarter Santa Anita Handicap, it was *Affirmed* first by four and a half lengths, with *Tiller* second, and *Exceller* gaining a dead-heat for show.

For ten weeks America's champion was away from competition, then raced in the Californian Stakes at Hollywood over a mile and a sixteenth. He carried 130 pounds and led all the way, winning by five lengths. In the Hollywood Gold Cup he carried 132 pounds, and it was the same story. The other horses simply could not get by him. The Gold Cup winner's purse of $275,000 raised *Affirmed*'s total earnings to the top of the all-time money winner's list. *Affirmed* had won over $2,000,000, replacing *Kelso* as the horse that had won the most.

From Hollywood Park, it was on to New York for a win in a one-mile exhibition race at Belmont. Then for the Marlboro Cup, *Affirmed* was assigned 133 pounds, 9 more than the current three-year-old champion *Spectacular Bid*. Barrera did not agree with only 124 pounds for the three-year-old and so failed to enter, an enormously complimentary judgement, for *Spectacular Bid* was far better, as they say, than an empty stall. The judgement was accurate, too, for *The Bid* won the Marlboro, won it easily.

Affirmed then raced in the weight-for-age Woodward on a track that was a sea of slop. As the mile and a quarter race was run, the big surprise had to be no *Affirmed* in the lead. At one point he was nowhere. All of a sudden in high gear, there he was, quickly closing the gap on the leaders. Moving through on the inside, Pincay, now his regular rider, didn't have to push. *Affirmed* had lots left.

Finally, *Affirmed* and *Spectacular Bid* did meet at Belmont for the Jockey Club Gold Cup. The weight-for-age race at a mile and a half was for a purse of $350,000. *Affirmed* had to put away the Belmont Stakes hero *Coastal*, then resist a strong move by Bill Shoemaker and *The Bid*. Such was *Affirmed*'s reputation that most people took a win for granted, but the true greatness of the moment could only be understood if *Spectacular Bid*'s presence was fully appreciated. Barrera knew how good he was; that's why he did not want *Affirmed* to give him 9 pounds in the Marlboro. *Spectacular Bid*, not *Alydar*, was probably the greatest horse *Affirmed* ever raced against. And in the Jockey Club Gold Cup, *Affirmed* won out by three-quarters of a length.

It was his last race, the last of twenty-nine, twenty-two of which he won, with total world-record earnings of $2,393,818. American racing was the beneficiary when the Wolfsons ran their Triple Crown three-year-old champion at four. They did what the *Seattle Slew* people did and what the *Spectacular Bid* people plan to do. They put *Affirmed*'s reputation into the hands of the handicappers. Their champion carried the weights, they gave weight away, and still they won.

Now his Florida breeding will be on the line with a $14,400,000 syndication. At $400,000 a share this chestnut son of *Exclusive Native* from the *Crafty Admiral* mare *Won't Tell You* is at stud at Leslie Combs II's Spendthrift Farm in Kentucky, another of America's brilliant stallions owned by more than twenty breeders.

Affirmed was America's Horse of the Year in 1978 and 1979, winning the Triple Crown in the first year and carrying top weight in the second. The third Triple Crown horse of the seventies, he was, like *Secretariat* and *Seattle Slew*, very much a television horse, thrilling millions who had never before experienced the excitement of thoroughbred racing. What set him apart in a decade of champions was the tenacity that he showed. So many of the great ones earned their reputations with easy wins or dramatic runs from far behind to win with style and a flourish. *Affirmed*, too, had his dramatic moments and he certainly had a style, but it was mostly the drama and style of struggling right down to the wire. He worked hard because he had to, and he earned the respect and admiration due a great champion.

Alleged

Vincent O'Brien is a familiar figure in the walking-rings of Europe. He is a man deeply involved with his work, though sometimes when he knows things are not right he has the appearance of someone who would give anything not to be there. Such was the case before the Arc de Triomphe when the undefeated *Nijinsky II* became horribly upset with the relentless antics of the ever-present photographers. Withdrawing further into his raincoat and brown hat, O'Brien could not hide his tension. In a way, it seemed as if through some secret communion he was trying to take his horse's burden onto himself. Perhaps this was not surprising, for in Ireland near Tipperary they'll tell you Vincent O'Brien can talk with horses. If you listen long enough they'll tell you horses can talk with O'Brien.

O'Brien's success began with jumpers in the late forties and early fifties. He won the Cheltenham Gold Cup three years in a row with *Cottage Rake* and the Champion Hurdles three years in a row with *Halton's Grace*. He won the Grand National, the world's most famous steeplechase, three consecutive years with *Early Mist, Royal Tan* and *Quare Times*. Soon after the *Quare Times* win in 1955, O'Brien gave up the jumpers for good and switched to the runners. His success continued on at the same phenomenal rate.

Ballymoss was his first big horse, winning the St. Leger at three then coming back to win the King George VI and the Prix de l'Arc de Triomphe. O'Brien won the Derby Stakes at Epsom five times with *Larkspur, Sir Ivor, Nijinsky II, Roberto* and *The Ministrel*, and his runners were continually being led into the winner's circle after the Irish Classics. The man became a legend.

Even for O'Brien, however, 1977 was a year that seemed too good to be true. He started by winning three great Classics with his Canadian *The Ministrel*: the English and Irish Derbies and the King George VI at Ascot. After a brief, brilliant campaign *The Ministrel* was syndicated and retired to stud at E.P. Taylor's Windfields Farm in Maryland, but O'Brien was still expected to take home all the money at the next great meet in the North at York. One upset after another spoiled his plans, the biggest of all being *Relkino* at 33–1 beating O'Brien's *Artaius* in the Benson and Hedges Gold Cup. There was one bright spot, however, and that was a performance by one of his horses that provided more than ample proof that the bottom had not fallen out of O'Brien's bucket of luck.

Alleged was the horse's name and, unlike most of the O'Brien runners at this particular meet at York, he was nothing short of remarkable. So remarkable, in fact, that on the strength of his one victory at York he was being declared the horse to beat in September at Doncaster in the St. Leger, third jewel in England's Triple Crown. The reason for all this speculation was *Alleged*'s splendid run in the Great Voltigeur Stakes at a mile and a half, his first ever start in a Classic.

Previously he had only been out in Ireland. At two he ran at the Curragh in a fifteen-runner maiden race over a distance of seven furlongs, and won by eight lengths. That was it for his two-year-old year. At three, he made three more Irish starts before coming to York, the first a ten-furlong race at Leopardstown which he won by two lengths. Then, back at the Curragh, he won the Royal Whip Stakes at a mile and a half at 33–1 and, at the same distance, the Gallinule Stakes. In this last start Lester Piggott was up for the first time, always a sign that a horse should get some very careful attention.

With Piggott in the saddle *Alleged* could never again be a longshot as he was in the Royal Whip Stakes. While Bill Shoemaker in the U.S. and Sandy Hawley in Canada enjoy similar fame and adulation, Piggott's place in British racing has many more sides. In the sixties and early seventies, the selection of favorites would often hinge on Piggott's choice of mounts in the Classics.

In 1968, for example, he chose to ride Raymond Guest's *Sir Ivor*, trained by O'Brien, in the Derby Stakes at Epsom, and his judgement was proved correct. *Sir Ivor* beat *Connaught*. But in the Irish Sweeps Derby, where *Sir Ivor* was still heavily favoured, the smart money was on Charles Engelhard's *Ribero*, trained by Fulke Johnson-Houghton, even though he had won only one race. The money was on *Ribero* because so was Piggott. At the end of the mile and a half Classic, *Ribero* crossed the wire two lengths ahead of *Sir Ivor*.

This uncanny ability to spot a winner has endeared Piggott, now Sir Lester, to millions of Britons. Even French racegoers are among his fans. They were jubilant when Piggott, after stealing jockey Alain Lequex's whip while passing him during the running of the Grand Prix de Deauville, replied to the stewards' accusations with the straight-faced reply, "I didn't steal the whip. I just borrowed it. As soon as I was finished with it I gave it back." The stewards, however, were not amused. They gave Piggott a twenty-day suspension.

In the Great Voltigeur Stakes Piggott had *Alleged* make all the running, shook him up with three furlongs to go, then went on to win by seven lengths. Horses are only as good as what they beat, and behind *Alleged*, far behind him, were *Classic Example* and *Lucky Sovereign*, both of whom had been less than two lengths behind *The Minstrel* in the Irish Derby, as well as *Hot Grove*, the colt that had been such a close second to *The Minstrel* in the English Derby. *Alleged* had run away and hidden, as they say, on the very same horses that *The Minstrel* had needed all of his strength to beat.

The speculation about the St. Leger was indeed well-founded, but at Doncaster the Queen's superb filly *Dunfermline* got the best of *Alleged* and beat him by just over a length. It was the only time *Alleged* ever saw another horse cross the finish line.

Despite the defeat in the St. Leger and despite the presence in the field of *Dunfermline*, *Alleged* commanded all the attention in the Prix de l'Arc de Triomphe three weeks later. Piggott judged him to be sharp enough to take over the lead after just three furlongs, with nine more to go. *Alleged* relished the task and maintained a steady pace. On the difficult run down the hill there was still no challenge. Where were *Dunfermline, Crow, Orange Bay* and *Dom Alaric*? When they came into the straight, with Piggott high up in his irons, *Alleged* still showed his heels. He seemed to accelerate, rendering his rivals powerless to close the gap on him. He crossed the line a length and a half in front of *Balmerino*. *Crystal Palace* was third, followed by *Dunfermline, Crow* and the rest. *Alleged* was the first three-year-old to win the Arc since *San San* in 1972. "The Wizard of Cashel", Vincent O'Brien had done it again. It was a fitting end to a magnificent year.

Early in the 1978 season it was announced that *Alleged* would race as a four-year-old. The King George VI and Queen Elizabeth Diamond Stakes and the Prix de l'Arc de Triomphe were to be his two main objectives. He started the season on May 12th at the Curragh, once more in the Royal Whip Stakes. He won over his four rivals easily, beating the second finisher *Irish Riddle* by two and a half lengths.

He missed the Coronation Cup at Epsom because the ground was too hard and would not suit him. Then O'Brien's stable was hit by a virus infection and it was decided to take no chances with *Alleged*. The decision to not race him was a wise one. O'Brien knew that a race could be too hard on him if he wasn't a hundred per cent right, and with his value increasing there was even less reason to gamble.

Despite making only one start in the season, however, *Alleged* was still very much in the news over the summer. He finally reappeared on September 17th at Longchamp in the mile and a quarter Prix du Prince d'Orange. He won from the French three-year-old *Louksor* by two and a half lengths without being driven, lowering the course record and putting himself into the role of favourite once again for the great Arc de Triomphe. O'Brien's eyes were twinkling over the rapid ground-devouring acceleration *Alleged* displayed when Piggott asked him.

On Arc day the ground was soft. Piggott decided to keep *Alleged* up with the first flight, never worse than third. When the field arrived in the straight *Alleged* moved away from the front runners and ran a catch-me-if-you-can race to the wire. Piggott, never resorting to the whip, hustled him along. The great acceleration was all there. The very good French mare *Trillion*, a huge horse, tried hard to get close, but her wonderful end-run was simply not good enough. She failed by two lengths.

It was a tremendous feat winning the Arc two years in a row, a feat not accomplished since *Alleged*'s paternal-great-grandsire *Ribot* scored the same rare double in 1955-56. With this victory in his last race, *Alleged* stood as the best mile and a half or middle distance horse in

Europe. And Vincent O'Brien looked like the best trainer in Europe. Once again he had demonstrated his uncanny knack for spotting talent and his ability to develop that talent to the full.

It wasn't surprising for O'Brien to have fancied *Alleged*. The success he had had with the Canadian *Nijinsky II* , the American *Roberto*, and most recently the new Canadian *The Minstrel* meant that there was always another stall for something promising from across the Atlantic.

Bred in America by Mrs. June McKnight, *Alleged* had been sold at the Keeneland Summer Sales for $34,000. As a two-year-old in training he had been sold again at the California Thoroughbred Breeders Association Sale for $175,000 to a syndicate, the main shareholder of which eventually was Britain's leading owner and sales bidder Robert Sangster.

Alleged was a wonderful looking bay colt by *Hoist the Flag* from a *Prince John* mare, *Princess Pout. Hoist the Flag* was by *Tom Rolfe*, and *Tom Rolfe* was by *Ribot*, first victorious in the Arc when O'Brien was winning his third Grand National with *Quare Times*.

Going back to the seventies and really placing *Hoist the Flag*, it is not difficult to assess the measure of his greatest son, *Alleged*. Not since the last American Triple Crown horse, *Citation* in 1948, had a horse been as exciting as *Hoist the Flag*. There were many who thought his main problem was that he was just too brilliant, winning six out of six, then losing one through a disqualification. He was a pre-race favourite for the 1971 Kentucky Derby, but shortly before the race he shattered his off-hind pastern. Fortunately, new surgical techniques allowed him to live and begin his career as a sire.

Both *Hoist the Flag* and *Alleged* had unbelievable bursts of speed when their riders asked for it, and *Alleged* also had the good fortune to be blessed with soundness.

After winning nine races in ten starts, *Alleged* was syndicated for $16,000,000, 40 shares at $400,000 each. He is now at stud at Walmac Farm in Lexington, Kentucky, another name to rank with those of the great champions trained by Vincent O'Brien.

Allez France

In Europe, *Sea-Bird* and *Ribot* are often called the horses of the century. So upon *Sea-Bird*'s retirement to stud in America the anticipation was phenomenal. Unfortunately, he failed to pass on his greatness until one day in September, 1972 there was a sign of something different. A beautifully turned out two-year-old filly with perfect conformation was led into the walking-ring. She was a bay, unraced, but unconcerned with the new routine. During the saddling her odds stayed steadily at even money. When Yves Saint-Martin arrived to ride her he seemed pleased to be with her. Saint-Martin's presence on a first time starter, a two-year-old filly, was sure to have influenced the odds, for he was the great French champion and the undisputed expert over the course at Longchamp.

People kept looking at this beautiful bay. She was a *Sea-Bird*, from a *Hail to Reason* mare named *Priceless Gem*, bred in Kentucky by a partnership named Bieber-Jacobs Stable, owned by the international sportsman Daniel Wildenstein and trained by Albert Klimscha. She was in with seven others and about to go a mile. Her name was *Allez France*.

On that first September day at Longchamp she won, drawing clear by two lengths. Then came the 1972 Arc de Triomphe Day on Sunday, October 8th. It was *San San* and Freddy Head's day, but much of the talk was about the *Sea-Bird*, the filly that won again for Saint-Martin in a sixteen-runner one-mile race called the Criterium des Pouliches. The race was for two-year-old fillies, and the best ones in training were in it. The *Sea-Bird* had only one horse beaten turning into the stretch. She was fifteen lengths behind the leaders, but when Saint-Martin asked her to run she got it all done inside the last furlong. They didn't call her the *Sea-Bird* anymore, they called her *Allez France*. And when they said her name they were excited because in this, her second start, she had beaten *Kerlande* and *Fiery Diplomat*, a winner of four straight.

In early 1973 she trained for the races like a champion. Her first start of the season was on April 29th at Longchamp in the Poule d'Essai des Pouliches, the French answer to the English One Thousand Guineas. There were eleven in it and all but the longshot *Muffy* and herself had already been racing. This time her race made the Arc Day "hair-raiser" look like a smart rehearsal. She started out just as hopelessly back behind the leaders. When they finally reached the short Longchamp straight she was not clear; she was badly trapped in seventh position and had nowhere to go. Suddenly, Saint-Martin spotted the narrowest of openings and asked her to go through. No sooner done than she was gone, galloping home an easy two and a half-length winner. *Princess Arjumand* was second, *Dahlia* third.

Allez France was now *Sea-Bird*'s first Classic winner, a true sign that something was different, that *Sea-Bird* at long last had a place as a sire. In fact, so strong was *Allez France*'s reputation after three undefeated starts that she was the favourite to beat the colts at Epsom in June. On May 13th she tried the colts for the first time in the Prix Lupin, an important French Derby Classic trial. The result was more than disappointing; she finished seventh. There was a difference of opinion in the usual post-mortem that follows such a disaster, for that's how it is regarded if an undefeated horse fails to make the board. Yves Saint-Martin blamed himself, but most people thought this was nonsense, that *Allez France* probably couldn't stay. So the Derby was abandoned, and the Prix de Diane at Chantilly became the new objective.

The Prix de Diane was a cavalry charge, with twenty-five runners on their way. *Allez France*, on the inside as the result of the draw, kept out of trouble and was guided into a position midway of the field. When Saint-Martin asked her she took over with ease, leaving *Dahlia* to finish second, *Virunga* third. The time of 2:07-2/5 was the fastest ever for the race.

Three months later, on September 3rd, she went off at 1–10 in the Prix de la Nonette for fillies at a distance of a mile and five-sixteenths. This time she had no rally for Saint-Martin and had to settle for fourth. *Gay Style, My Great Aunt* and *Snobishness* beat her, and maybe lack of conditioning did too, because three weeks later Saint-Martin got her going in the Prix Vermeille at a mile and a half and she won easily, coming at the end with a great run. This at least ended the speculation about her not being able to stay.

On October 7th at Longchamp she started in the Prix de l'Arc de Triomphe, Europe's greatest Classic, also at a mile and a half. *Allez France* had never looked better than before the Arc, and she commanded much attention in the huge walking-ring. She faced twenty-seven runners in what appeared to be a fairly formidable task, because some of them were the best mile and half runners in training. The filly *San San*, who had won the Arc one year before, and *Dahlia* were both in it, but they weren't at their best. *Allez France* went off at almost 9–5 and managed a most courageous second two and a half lengths behind *Rheingold*, who was simply too good for her.

To end the 1973 season her connections shipped her to Newmarket for the mile and a quarter Champion Stakes. At 3–2 odds she managed another second, this time to *Hurry Harriet* whom she had beaten at Longchamp. Over the season she had started seven times, won three, finished second in two, and was unplaced in two. Her trainer Albert Klimscha retired at the end of the season, and was replaced by Angel Penna.

Penna was Argentina's and Venezuela's leading trainer before racing in the United States where he handled *Bold Reason* and *Czar Alexander*. His first season in France was in 1972 and it was quite a debut. He won the Prix Mornay with *Filiberto*, the Poule d'Essai des Pouliches with *Mata Hari*, and the Prix Vermeille and Prix de l'Arc de Triomphe with the filly *San San*. In 1974 he started training the Wildenstein stable horses including the great one, *Allez France*.

Penna started her three times in six weeks. The first was on April 15th at the Prix d'Harcourt. She led throughout, winning the mile and a quarter Longchamp race easily by three lengths. The English colt *Tsar* was second, *Mister Six Top* third, and *Dahlia* fourth. As is often the case,

the Prix d'Harcourt was used as a prep race for the Prix Ganay on May 5th. The going was soft for the mile and five-sixteenths race, but *Allez France* seemed to move up on it, winning with great ease by five lengths. *Tennyson* was second and *Gombas* third, while *Dahlia* was a distant fifth. *Allez France* had now met *Dahlia* six times and had beaten her every time.

On June 30th she ran in the Prix d'Ispahan at nine furlongs. The Longchamp course was again rated as soft. She raced absolutely, as they say in North America, far back. But when the six runners ahead of her turned into the straight Saint-Martin went to work on her. She had a fifteen-length lead to cut down and catch, but she finally got to the front in the final eighth in a spectacular display that showed the great confidence her jockey had in her. It was a demanding race, the kind that trainers like Horatio Luro really dread. As Luro once said, "A horse is so much like a lemon, and so every time you squeeze it you get a little more juice, but you never can put it back, because it is gone."

Penna now put *Allez France* away until September 6th when she started in the Prix Foy at a mile and three-eighths. Saint-Martin let her trail her small field of three other rivals and then he asked her. It was an easy win over the soft going and stood her in good stead for another try at the Arc on October 6th.

With twenty runners accepted, she went off as the 1–2 favourite and gave everyone the thrill they were waiting for. There was heightened drama before the Arc because ten days earlier Yves Saint-Martin had suffered a small broken bone at the top of his thigh as a result of being thrown in the paddock at Maisons-Laffitte. At one point in the pre-Arc stories, Lester Piggott was to be the rider on *Allez France*, but Saint-Martin deemed himself fit to dress following an injection of some pain killer. It's always a good sign when a jockey is almost desperate to ride a certain horse.

Allez France drew the number fifteen stall, an outside one resulting in Saint-Martin deciding to wait rather than try to save ground on the inside. Such tactics could have failed because her style as the Queen of Europe's middle distance runners was to stay far back then move between horses. With just half a mile to go she made a very fast move on the outside of her field, so fast that the momentum carried her quickly to the front turning into the straight. Once in command she seemed secure until *Comtesse de Loir*, hard-ridden, boldly challenged her. The two went at it for about 300 feet with *Allez France* holding her stout challenger even, then gamely beating her by a short head. It was a spectacular finish to a great season consisting of five starts and five wins. Greatness for a mare must surely be earned by racing more than two seasons and in races that aren't restricted to fillies. *Allez France* had now earned all the honours.

As a five-year-old she had things all to herself at the beginning, winning her first two starts with ease. But on June 29th she failed to rally and finished third, two lengths behind the winner. These three races, all at Longchamp, were the Prix Ganay, the Prix Dallas and the Prix d'Ispahan which she had won the year before. Following the same pattern he had used the previous season, Penna put her away until September, then brought her out for an easy win in the Prix Foy at a mile and three-eighths. If horses could talk maybe they would say when enough is enough. In three more races, her last three, she was clearly not quite the *Allez France* of 1974.

At just under 9–5 she went down to defeat in the Arc, finishing a disappointing fifth, eight and a half lengths behind the winner *Star Appeal*. She had a rough trip in the 1975 running, lacking room at one point and having to be restrained as a result. The sudden slowing down caused a horse running behind her to run up on her hind heels. She suffered a cut, lost a shoe, and must have wondered what was going on. When she returned to be unsaddled she looked very tired, and Saint-Martin looked very disappointed. It was far from her best, and her last ever race in France.

She ran two weeks later in the Champion Stakes at Newmarket and beat the Arc winner *Star Appeal*, but lost to the much improved filly *Rose Bowl* by a length and a half. Unfortunately for her form, she was then flown to Los Angeles for a try at Santa Anita's $350,000 National Championship Invitational Handicap.

The big race was run over the main Santa Anita dirt track at a distance of one mile and a quarter, track fast. Yves Saint-Martin, who had ridden her in every one of her races, also flew out to the American west coast. They went off at nearly 7–1, the first time they hadn't been favoured. A good many people must have known something, for *Allez France* finished eleventh, last in the eleven-horse field.

She raced twenty-one times in all, seventeen times at the magnificent Longchamp course in Paris, once at Chantilly, twice at Newmarket in England and once at Santa Anita in the United States, appearing on these famous tracks over four seasons. She would have travelled more, but she did not ship well. Even so, she won thirteen races and $1,386,146.

As a broodmare *Allez France* encountered severe difficulties in the early part of her career. In the first year she was bred to *Secretariat* and sadly delivered a dead foal. She was not bred back the next year, and when in the third year she was bred to *Northern Dancer* she came up barren. In 1979 she was bred to *Seattle Slew*, who also resides at Spendthrift, and in the early spring of the new decade produced a beautiful filly who fearlessly races around her paddock, carefully watched by her proud mum.

Today at Spendthrift Farm in Lexington, you'll often see a band of broodmares suddenly move as one. *Allez France* will always be their leader. She's big and tough and in the nineteen seventies was the greatest mare in the world.

Dahlia

There is something very special about winning on foreign soil. The experience and all that goes with it is as old as racing itself. What great times the jubilant Irish must have had after putting one over on the English at Epsom. Then there were the cross-Channel invasions of the British at Deauville or Longchamp and the French at Ascot, and the transatlantic excursions of both French and British to Belmont, Woodbine and Laurel. Nelson Bunker Hunt of Dallas, Texas had this experience with three top horses that raced in France and England before coming home to America. The outstanding mare *Dahlia* was among them.

Dahlia was bred in Kentucky. She was a chestnut by *Vaguely Noble* from the *Honeys Alibi* mare, *Charming Alibi,* a foal of 1970. At two she was sent to Maurice Zilber's stable at Chantilly and quickly made friends with everyone, though she was not easy to train and was often more than difficult in her races where she showed from the start that patience was not one of her virtues. She pulled hard and was often troublesome over any efforts to settle her down. Relaxing was something she could rarely do.

In her first race as a two-year-old, Lester Piggott had the mount in a five-furlong sprint at Longchamp on September 10, 1972. The best she could manage was fifth in a six-horse field. She had her second start on October 26th in the one-mile Prix des Reservoirs for fillies and Bill Pyers actually got her to the front at midstretch, but she failed to stay, losing to *Begora.* It was a good effort, despite the odds of 15–1 against her. Two starts, one a sprint and one at a mile, won't tell everything, but they can point the way. *Dahlia* looked like a good prospect for the filly races at three, and Bill Pyers seemed to suit her rather difficult ways.

So on April 8, 1973 she started with Pyers in the Prix de la Grotte. She faced ten other fillies and made a late rally to win going away by three-quarters of a length, rewarding her backers with a good 7–1 return. In her second three-year-old start she raced evenly, but ran third on soft turf, again at a mile. Then, on May 20th, asked to go ten furlongs in Longchamp's Prix Saint-Alary, she drew clear over *Virunga* and *Kashara*. The Paris punters still did not believe in her; she paid off at 5–1. In her next start, the Prix de Diane (French Oaks), the going was good over the mile and five-sixteenths and Pyers got her up for second. She moved well, but she was just no match for the favourite, the great *Allez France* with Yves Saint-Martin.

Now she crossed the Channel to the British Isles and showed what she could really do. On July 21st she raced in the Irish Guinness Oaks at the Curragh over a mile and a half, drawing away to win for Pyers to the sound of Irish cheers. In her wake by three lengths was the champion *Mysterious* who had earlier won both the English One Thousand Guineas and the Epsom Oaks.

Seven days later she faced a strong field in the King George VI and Queen Elizabeth Stakes at Ascot. Again the distance was a mile and a half, but this time the race was not restricted to fillies, nor limited to three-year-olds. Among her eleven rivals were *Roberto* with Lester Piggott, *Rheingold* with Yves Saint-Martin and *Scottish Rifle* with Ron Hutchinson. *Dahlia* was in with many of the top ones, but it made no difference to her. She moved boldly three furlongs from the finish and simply drew away with ease, leaving the four-year-old *Rheingold* behind by six lengths. Pyers' smiles matched those of canny Maurice Zilber as she was led into the winner's circle. The price was right at 10–1. As Zilber has said, "I know very well how to take money out of the track."

These wins helped the Paris punters figure her out, for in her start in the Prix Niel at Longchamp she paid off at only 9–10 after winning by half a length. She was the favourite again in the Prix Vermeille, but the best she could do was a fifth-place finish, beaten again by *Allez France* and pulling a leg muscle in the bargain. She lost again, and lost badly, in the Prix de l'Arc de Triomphe where she finished sixteenth in a field of twenty-seven, beaten by nineteen lengths. She was 8–1 and, interestingly enough, the winner was *Rheingold,* with *Allez France* second.

But she ended the season in a big way when Zilber shipped her to North America to run in the Washington, D.C. International in November. The course was yielding, but *Dahlia* loved it. *London Company* led for seven furlongs, then *Tentam* took over the lead in the stretch. *Scottish Rifle* and *Big Spruce* both became dangerous, but *Dahlia* and Pyers had a perfect race, relaxing early, saving ground, then moving between horses and finally going with an explosive rally to win under brisk handling. Her wins in four countries were enough for *Dahlia* to be voted Horse of the Year in Europe, the first filly to be so honoured.

Her four-year-old season started badly. She made only one start a month in the first three months and failed to win each time. Pyers rode her in all three. Yves Saint-Martin then took over and she finally found the winner's circle, first in the Grand Prix de Saint-Cloud where, suprisingly, she led most of the way.

But her finest moment came in the King George VI and Queen Elizabeth Stakes, the highlight of the July meet at Ascot. First run in 1951, the King George VI had never been won by the same horse twice. *Dahlia* came over from France to try for the double. For the first time since her two-year-old debut Lester Piggott was back in the saddle. At the start *Dahlia* and Piggott stayed far back, biding their time, while her stablemate *Hippodamia* kept the field honest with a fast pace. Coming out of the final turn, the leaders were *Hippodamia, Snow Knight,* the Derby winner, and *Buoy,* a top English middle-distance runner. Piggott moved *Dahlia* up to fourth without any urging whatsoever. Going into the straight her contenders were all flat-out, but in no time at all she went from fourth to first to win in a canter two and a half lengths in front of the One Thousand Guineas winner, *Highclere.* It was a powerful run accomplished with almost ridiculous ease against some of the best in training.

This great performance was soon matched by her race at the rich York meet where she won the mile and five-sixteenths Benson and Hedges Gold Cup, again by two and a half lengths. *Imperial Prince* was second, *Snow Knight* third. After a third-place finish in the Prix du Prince d'Orange on September 15th, Zilber shipped her again to North America to end the season with three major races.

In the first, the Man o'War at Belmont, she won ridden out for Ronnie Turcotte. *Krafty Khale* was second, *London Company* third. Then Lester Piggott flew over to ride her in the mile and five-eighths Canadian International Championship Stakes.

The Canadian International is an example of how keen the competition became for name horses in the seventies, and of how track operators did their utmost to lure the very best. It was first run as the Long Branch Championship for three-year-olds in 1938 on the dirt at the old Long Branch track. The winner's purse won by *Bunty Lawless* was $2,125. The 1979 running on the Marshall turf course at Toronto's Woodbine carried a guaranteed purse of $200,000, with $120,000 going to the winner, *Golden Act.*

In the early days the greats of Canadian racing galloped home to fame and glory, if not fortune; greats like *Bunty Lawless, Sir Marlboro, Shepperton, Kingarvie* and *Canada's Teddy.* There were also good American-bred 'Canadian' horses like *Arise,* who also won Saratoga's historic Travers, and *Bull Page,* the Bull Lea horse who later sired *Flaming Page,* a Queen's Plate winner and the dam of the great *Nijinsky II.* But except for *He's A Smoothie* and *George Royal,* one of the great horses of Canadian racing who won in 1966 and 1967, the Championship was for years an American berry patch. The Americans continued to dominate in the early seventies, arriving with *Secretariat* in 1973. Needless to say, the pot had been greatly sweetened for the occasion, and the beautiful chestnut did not disappoint, scampering home by six and a half lengths for a purse of $92,755. Through the rest of the seventies, the Internationalists came to win, including *Snow Knight* and *Yonth. Dahlia* started the trend.

London Company and *Big Spruce* shipped in from Belmont and, with the English Derby winner *Snow Knight,* made it a good field. Nine horses went to the post, with *Dahlia* the odds-on choice at 1–2. At the start *Snow Knight* with Sandy Hawley up went to the front, at one stage leading by ten lengths. *Protectora* raced second, *Carney's Point* third, while *Dahlia* and *Big Spruce* were well back. *Dahlia* stayed in until the far turn where she moved up off the hedge. In a bold move she came between horses rounding the turn and a furlong out burst into the lead to win smartly by a length. *Big Spruce* came up for second and *Carney's Point* held on for third.

Piggott rode her again at Laurel in November, but this time wasn't so lucky, for he lost too much ground entering the stretch and was beaten by a length and a half. The French invader *Admetus* was the winner at 33–1. Despite the loss, *Dahlia* was still voted best turf horse in America for 1974.

It was her last big year. In 1975 she raced eleven times, travelling from France to England, back to France, then on to Toronto and Laurel. She managed to win only once, the Benson and Hedges at York which she had won the year before. When she made her annual trip to North America, Piggott, one of the shrewdest judges of form in the business, decided to stay at home. Once again his judgement was proved correct. *Dahlia* with Hawley was fourth in the Canadian Championship in Toronto, with *Snow Knight* the winner, and in the Washington, D.C. International she beat only one horse in a field of nine.

Now she was in North America to stay. As a six-year-old she was turned over to the great California trainer Charles Whittingham who found her to be still temperamental, but a willing mare in training. He said she wasn't what he would call a pretty mare, but added that she had a nice head, great shoulders, was big at the withers and a little over at the knee. She still ran best when covered up, kept just in behind the other horses so that when she was moved out with a clear space ahead, she knew it was time to run. "As soon as she could see daylight, she'd go. Wish I had had more like her". She won two races for him at Hollywood Park, one of them the rich Hollywood Invitational Turf Handicap. But it was all she could do as a six-year-old to win two in thirteen starts.

For two full seasons she was brilliant, with her greatest moments at Ascot and Woodbine. Other than her arch-rival *Allez France* there was no mare in the seventies to compare with her. No filly equalled her Horse of the Year honour.

Now at Nelson Bunker Hunt's Bluegrass Farm in Kentucky she is loved as she was in training at Maurice Zilber's yard in Chantilly. Her foals so far have all been colts. Her first, by the game little Kentucky Derby and Belmont Stakes winner *Bold Forbes,* was named *Indomitable.* He is now with Maurice Zilber in France and the word is out that he could be a good one. Her second foal was by *What A Pleasure,* and in 1980 she is due to have her third by *J.O. Tobin,* England's champion two-year-old. She will then be bred to *Lyphard,* the *Northern Dancer* stud who sired the heroine of the 1979 Arc *Three Troikas.* Wherever they go *Dahlia's* foals will be carefully watched, always the case when a mare was a Classic champion.

Exceller

He was a good horse anywhere. He proved that by winning eleven Group I races in six seasons. He was as good as any I've ever trained.'' Trainer Charles Whittingham said this not long ago at Santa Anita about *Exceller*, one of the great horses that raced in the nineteen seventies. Of all those horses he probably got the least recognition, yet in a sense he was one of the horses that did the most.

He·was a Kentucky-bred by *Vaguely Noble* from the *Bald Eagle* mare *Too Bold.* Mrs. Charles W. Engelhard, his breeder, consigned him to the Keeneland Summer Sales and he was knocked down to Nelson Bunker Hunt for only $25,000. He was one of several horses that Hunt eventually moved from trainer Maurice Zilber's care to the yard of Francois Mathet.

Exceller made his first start in a maiden race at Deauville on August 10, 1975, and finished eighth in a field of twelve. He then started twice on the soft going at Evry, winning both races, but being disqualified in one for causing interference. His fourth and final start at two was at Longchamp where he ran well and finished third over a soft mile and a quarter. He ran best from behind, preferring to rally with a good late run towards the finish.

In this early part of his career, he was greatly upstaged by his more promising stablemates *Empery* and *Youth*. This situation continued into *Exceller*'s three-year-old year, at least into June of 1976, particularly when *Empery* won the English Derby at Epsom and *Youth* followed by winning the Prix du Jockey Club, the French Derby at Chantilly. They were syndicated for $6,000,000 each, then distinguished themselves in a chilling way by losing, *Empery* losing the Irish Sweeps Derby to *Malacate*, and

Youth finishing 'nowhere' in the King George VI and Queen Elizabeth Diamond Stakes at Ascot.

Exceller now came into his own, not in the big glamour races, but in the gruelling Grand Prix de Paris and in the Prix Royal Oak, two Longchamp races both at a mile and fifteen-sixteenths. He won both by a margin of four lengths, revealing the stamp of a very classy stayer. Before these two important victories he had managed a good second at Longchamp, a two and a half-length win at Evry, and a six-length win at Chantilly. But at the end of his three-year-old season, he finished a shocking nineteenth out of twenty in the Prix de l'Arc de Triomphe. The stewards were so suspicious that they ordered special testing for any evidence of pre-race tampering. Tranquilizing big horses before important races is one way of stopping them, but in *Exceller*'s case nothing was found.

As a four-year-old in 1977, *Exceller* continued to improve. He started in France, England, Canada and the United States. Mathet still trained him until the North American trip, then Maurice Zilber took over. *Exceller* started his four-year-old year at Saint-Cloud, but he was no threat. At Longchamp on May 1st he really turned it on for the Prix Ganay, finishing a strong second to *Arctic Tern*, and one month later beat *Quiet Fling* by a neck in the Coronation Cup at Epsom over a mile and a half, a distance he had handled with ease the year before at Chantilly.

Then came two of the three top European races for older horses, the Grand Prix de Saint-Cloud and the King George VI and Queen Elizabeth Diamond Stakes at Ascot. On July 3rd, he was at Saint-Cloud. His regular rider,

George Dubroeucq, was there too, but not to ride *Exceller*. Dubroeucq chose *Diagramatic* because he thought a morning workout between the two horses meant something. All it meant was that *Diagramatic* could beat *Exceller* in the morning, for *Exceller* with Freddy Head got up to win by a neck, while *Diagramatic* finished seventh.

On July 23rd, *Exceller* met ten other runners for the great Ascot prize. *The Minstrel,* who had won both the English and Irish Derbies that year, won a desperately fought final yards finish over *Orange Bay.* Lester Piggott's saddle artistry was never more evident, for he had *The Minstrel* stretched to the limit. But Freddy Head and *Exceller* finished third after a tremendous rush, only a length and a half behind the first two.

It was his last start in Europe. But before the year was over, *Exceller* made four starts in North America in the short space of six weeks. They were all on grass and, except for his Toronto race, all at a mile and a half. He was now following in the hoof-prints of his former stablemates *Dahlia* and *Youth,* for Maurice Zilber was back. In the Man o'War at Belmont, *Exceller* and Angel Cordero Jr. got into enough trouble to lose it all, but managed to finish second to *Majestic Light.* Zilber, unsatisfied, wanted another chance and he soon got it, not in New York, but in Toronto. Both *Exceller* and *Majestic Light* were nominated for the Canadian International Championship Stakes, along with *Johnny D* and nine others.

The mile and five-furlong course was soft, almost water-logged after incessant rain. Sandy Hawley kept *Majestic Light* on the outside fairly close to the leaders; Cordero kept *Exceller* back and waited, even when Hawley made his move to the front. *Exceller* raced like a plodder, then on the lower part of the last bend he turned it on. In the stretch he suddenly accelerated and ran like a sprinter in a great burst that carried him past *Majestic Light* to win by a length. *Johnny D,* a formidable runner just now developing, was third. It was a powerful run that would be repeated in both Los Angeles and New York, but not in 1977.

He started twice more that year over the same course conditions and against the same rivals as in Toronto, but he had simply gone right off form. At Laurel he lost the Washington, D.C. International by seventeen lengths. *Johnny D* was first, *Majestic Light* second. Lester Piggott came over to ride him in Aqueduct's Turf Classic and he was beaten by twenty-two lengths. *Johnny D, Majestic Light* and *Crow* were the first three across the line.

At the age of five in 1978, he ran his best campaign. He was now under the care of Charles Whittingham in California. He arrived in the west much the worse for

wear, but came around and showed what he could do by winning the ten-furlong Arcadia Handicap over the main dirt course. He missed winning the San Luis Rey by a length on firm turf, but Whittingham had him ready for the San Juan Capistrano, the rich closing feature of Santa Anita's big winter meet. Parading in the walking-ring, he radiated good health and conditioning. In the race *Noble Dancer* and Steve Cauthen made all the pace, holding off first *Text* then *Copper Mel,* but not *Exceller* whom Bill Shoemaker brought on steadily from a good place in the middle of the field to finally win by a neck.

He followed up with four starts at the Hollywood Park meet, losing the Century Handicap with Don Pierce up, but coming back for three important victories, all with Bill Shoemaker. The first was the Hollywood Invitational Turf Handicap where he carried 127 pounds over the firm turf and won in 2:25-4/5, 1/5 off the course record. He moved between horses willingly, closed courageously and won with two and a half lengths in hand. In the $350,000 Hollywood Gold Cup, ten furlongs on the dirt, he got up by a neck on the wire, though he was actually going away and in a few more strides would have been clear. Back on the Hollywood turf course in the $150,000 Sunset Handicap, he ran far back, overcame trouble, and with an excellent ground-saving ride by 'The Shoe' carried his top weight of 130 pounds on to victory over *Diagramatic* and *Effervescing.* Three wins in four starts in twelve weeks said it all. *Exceller* was a rare horse in the peak of condition, and it was now time for a try at the Big Apple in New York.

He crossed the country with no bother to start in two races, the first of which was the $150,000 Woodward Stakes. The Belmont track was fast, but so was *Seattle Slew* who ran the mile and a quarter in a new track record time of 2:00 flat. *Exceller* was four lengths behind, over six lengths to the good of the third-place finisher *It's Freezing.* Two weeks later came the challenging $300,00 Jockey Club Gold Cup.

The finest horses in American racing – *Man o'War, Gallant Fox, War Admiral, Whirlaway, Citation, Nashua, Kelso, Buckpasser* and *Forego* – have won the Jockey Club Gold Cup. *Kelso* won it in five consecutive years. Its history is one of the best in the country, and the 61st running carried on the great tradition. It was a mile and a half under the wettest, sloppiest Belmont dirt conditions ever seen. Best of all, for the first time ever, two winners of the Triple Crown met – *Affirmed* and *Seattle Slew.*

Seattle Slew was the favourite and broke from the gate first, going to the front to the cheers of thousands of supporters. *Affirmed* with Cauthen was right after him.

Around the first turn *Affirmed*'s saddle slipped, but still he chased his rival until the far turn when Cauthen could no longer do him any justice. Cordero on *Seattle Slew* momentarily lost an iron, but he kept *'The Slew'* in front and began to race away. Then all of a sudden a horse from the off-the-pace group emerged second and rapidly cut down *Seattle Slew*'s lead. It was *Exceller* running like a wild horse. Shoemaker said the going was so bad and the visibility so poor that when he was back in the small pack he couldn't see a thing. *Exceller* picked up speed on his own, so Shoemaker let him run. Coming up to the stretch, he drew up alongside *'The Slew'* and as they turned for home the Belmont stands erupted. Through the stretch *Exceller* inched forward until they reached the eighth pole. The others were seven behind and out of it. *Exceller* now had *'The Slew'*, was in front by half a length. But *Seattle Slew* was strong. He fought back, and the gap narrowed again. Now *Exceller* was in trouble. *'The Slew'* was coming, coming in a devastating way that looked invincible. But inside those last few terrible yards, *Exceller* managed to hold on by a nose, managed to hold off the toughest, fastest, classiest horse in training.

Exceller was to win only one more race, the Oak Tree Invitational the following November 5th. As a six-year-old he raced four times, but came close only once, finishing second to *Tiller* after getting to the front in the 1979 San Juan Capistrano. In his last race, at Hollywood Park with Sandy Hawley up, he finished third and pulled up lame with a broken coffin bone. Fortunately, he recovered and was retired to stud at Gainesway Farm near Lexington, Kentucky.

From two to six *Exceller* started in thirty-three races, winning sixteen times and earning a staggering $1,569,002. As a five-year-old in 1978, he won seven times in ten starts, with six of the wins in Group 1 races. In that year alone his earnings totalled $879,790.

Six of his winning races were at a mile and a half, five were over the turf courses of Chantilly, Epsom, Hollywood and Santa Anita. The dirt that came up into his face never stopped him, nor did the soft, tiring grass under his hooves. Not even the slop could slow him down in the memorable struggle with *Seattle Slew*. That day at Belmont had to be his greatest moment. Only a true champion could have triumphed in such a test.

Forego,

a great gelding, was three times American Horse of the Year.

Grundy,

a Derby Stakes winner, was the best horse Peter Walwyn ever trained.

Mill Reef,

a hero in England's Derby and France's Arc, was as courageous as they come.

The Minstrel,

sired by *Northern Dancer*, was a winner at Ascot in a tour de force run.

Forego

Forego never forgets the sound of the races. Every time the field heads down the neighbouring Keeneland backstretch he starts to rebel, for he wants to be there. His battered forelegs and the faraway look in his eyes say it all. *Forego* has been there. He can never return.

"He had a look of eagles…"

That was trainer Peter Walwyn's first impression of *Grundy* at the sales – that and his unfashionable colour, a washy chestnut with flaxen mane and tail. He describes *Grundy* as 'a very well-proportioned horse who looks smaller than he actually is, deep and thickset, with an almost classic Arab head and legs like iron.'

Even today, Grundy still plays like a precocious two-year-old

Walwyn found Grundy to have tremendous character and to be extremely boisterous. As a result, he took two months to break in, rather than the normal month. From then on *Grundy* was easy to train. He proved to be a very keen student, always alert and observant.

Paul Mellon's Mill Reef

Mill Reef is so close to perfection in repose or in motion it is hard to believe that metal plates are holding the left foreleg in place.

With his great intelligence, *Mill Reef* spared himself after undergoing leg surgery. It probably saved his life. Now, with *Grundy*, he can enjoy The National Stud Farm paddocks at Newmarket.

"Like a little boy out of school…"

As soon as he is turned out,
The Minstrel's favourite trick is
to quickly wriggle out of his
halter. This little Houdini routine
is always good for an extra
fifteen minutes before his amused
handlers can bring him in.

Forego

The Thoroughbred Racing Association's annual Eclipse Awards Dinner, alternating between the east and west coasts, is to American thoroughbred racing what "Oscar" night is to American filmmaking. It is the night to honour racing's champions of the year. The winners are determined by a combined poll comprising people from the board of selection of the Thoroughbred Racing Association of North America, the Daily Racing Form, and the National Turf Writers Association.

At the fourth annual dinner at San Francisco's Fairmont Hotel, Martha Gerry proudly accepted three awards for her great gelding *Forego* – the sprinting, the handicap and the Horse of the Year honours. The highlight of the fifth dinner at New York's Waldorf Astoria was Martha Gerry accepting two Eclipse Awards to the sustained cheers and applause of 1,100 people. *Forego* had won the handicap and Horse of the Year awards again. At the sixth annual dinner at Los Angeles' Century Plaza emotions ran high, because in 1976 the huge gelding had done it again. Martha Gerry stole the show once more as for the third straight year *Forego* was named handicap champion and Horse of the Year. In 1977, at the age of seven, he lost out in the Horse of the Year voting to the sensational *Seattle Slew*, but did win the handicap championship again, his fourth best colt or gelding (four-year-old and up) honour in a row.

The Eclipse Awards have only been presented since 1971, but no matter how long they last *Forego*'s fame as a winner of eight will maintain a standard of excellence that cannot be ignored.

Forego's story is the story of weight. People outside the world of racing often don't understand how a few pounds off and a few pounds on can make such a difference between winning and losing. But, just as a bag of groceries with a few extra cans seems to weigh more the closer one gets to home, so those few extra pounds carried by a horse begin to tell shortly before the finish wire, particularly after a distance of ground has been covered. In the seventies, *Forego* carried more pounds than any of his rivals and still managed to cross the wire in front. He was American racing's weight-carrier supreme.

A foal of 1970, *Forego* was big, very big, and seemed even greater than the seventeen hands he became. His sire was the South American import *Forli*, a stallion that Martha Gerry had bought a share in, and his dam was a *Hasty Road* mare named *Lady Golconda*.

He started his career as a three-year-old in Florida in 1973, finishing second to *Royal and Regal* in Gulfstream's Florida Derby. He was the beaten favourite at 2 – 1. At one point at the top of the stretch, it looked like he might win, but *Forego* couldn't always follow through in his first year. He also had not yet perfected the style of running that would soon lead him to the winner's circle.

In the Kentucky Derby, as a 28 – 1 shot in his only Triple Crown race effort, he ended up on the inside, managed to hit the rail entering the far turn, then raced extremely wide coming into the stretch to finish fourth, eleven lengths behind *Secretariat*. He followed up with a third in Belmont's one-mile Withers Stakes on May 30th. It was proving to be an uneven year.

In the late fall and early winter, however, the combination of *Forego* and jockey Heliodoro Gustines finally began to pay off, first at New York's Aqueduct in the Jerome Handicap at a mile. *Forego* carried 124 pounds and finished second to *Step Nicely*, with 118 pounds, in a race run in the Jerome record time of 1:34. It was a good effort, and the next two were even better. He won both the Roamer Handicap at a mile and three-sixteenths and the Discovery Handicap at nine furlongs, carrying 127 pounds to victory in the Discovery. *Forego* was a proven weight-carrier in his own three-year-old division. The 1973 year in America belonged to *Secretariat*, but *Forego* managed to make a mark by winning nine of his eighteen starts and $188,909. Best of all, he looked like a horse with a future.

And what a future! *Forego* at four quickly became an undisputed champion. He could sprint and go a distance, any distance. He could do it with the best and with big weights up, always giving away pounds to his rivals. For nine months from February 9th at Florida's Gulfstream to November 9th at New York's Aqueduct, *Forego's* fantastic finishes were the talk of the sport. He raced thirteen times and won eight, finished second in two, third in two, and unplaced in one for earnings of $545,086.

Again, he started the season in Florida. He carried 125 pounds in the nine-furlong Donn Handicap at Gulfstream and won over the good little five-year-old *True Knight* (123 pounds), serving notice that he'd be awfully tough in the races to come. Two weeks later he carried top weight of 127 pounds in the ten-furlong Gulfstream Park Handicap. Heliodoro Gustines, sensing his greatness, took him back immediately after the start and held on to him strongly until he had dropped far back. He raced along wide with plenty in reserve to the second turn where he started to move. On the final turn he picked up the tiring *Strictly Business*, then, with some urging, held off *True Knight* (123 pounds) to win by half a length.

A month later he carried high weight of 129 pounds in Hialeah's famous ten-furlong Widner Handicap and ran much the same race as the Gulfstream Handicap. He was taken far back after the start and didn't make a move until the field had gone five furlongs. He then picked it up and caught *Play The Field* on the final turn. Once again Gustines kept him good and wide and gave him a few reminders to keep going. He won by a length over *True Knight* and *Play The Field*, who just lasted for third.

With a three-for-three record in Florida, *Forego* moved on to New York for the big handicaps in the summer and fall. As a sharpener, he carried 129 pounds in Belmont's Carter Handicap in May. There was nothing unusual about the high weight, but there certainly was about the distance, for the Carter was only seven furlongs, one of America's important sprints. It didn't matter to *Forego*. He won with a flourish in 1:22-1/5. Now he was ready for

New York's major summer races for older horses, the Metropolitan Handicap at Belmont and the Brooklyn Handicap and Suburban Handicap, both at Aqueduct.

In the one-mile Metropolitan *Forego* had to carry 134 pounds. He ran a game race and finished second to the fast-closing *Arbees Boy* who carried only 112 pounds and shocked the punters by paying off at 60–1. There was a terrible silence that seemed to have its own sound that day. After a good second-place finish in the seven-furlong Nassau County Handicap, *Forego* was set for the Brooklyn on the Fourth of July. Gustines kept him back until the far turn, then moved him up quickly on the outside for a duel through the stretch with the sharp Boston invader *Billy Come Lately*. *Forego* won by three-quarters of a length in 1:54-4/5 for the mile and three-sixteenths, with *Billy Come Lately* second and his Metropolitan conqueror *Arbees Boy* third. *Forego* had carried 129 pounds, giving 15 pounds to *Billy Come Lately* and 13 to *Arbees Boy*. *Forego* again carried high weight of 131 pounds in the ten-furlong Suburban. *True Knight*, now at the top of his form, was in with 127. During the running *Forego* waited for three-quarters of a mile then ran the last half. It was a game effort and he finished third, a length and a quarter behind *True Knight* and the second-place finisher *Plunk*, a speed horse from California. So his score for the three New York summer handicaps was a second, a first and a third. He gave weight away in all of them.

Beginning in September, *Forego* took on another three-race series in New York that had become all important: the Marlboro Cup Handicap at nine furlongs, the Woodward Stakes at a mile and a half and the Jockey Club Gold Cup Stakes at two miles.

In the Marlboro on September 14th, the track was sloppy and Gustines felt his mount simply could not get going. *Forego*, assigned 126 pounds, once again couldn't deliver a strong stretch drive. He finished third behind *Big Spruce* with 120 pounds and *Arbees Boy* with 119. But he didn't have to give weight away on September 18th in the Woodward at Belmont, for the Woodward was not a handicap at that time, but a weight-for-age race in which three-year-olds were assigned 119 pounds, older horses 126 pounds. Champions were not penalized; they were all in at equal weights on the scale. The track was fast and *Forego* found the conditions to his liking, but he still had to work to win. He had only one horse beaten in the eleven-horse field after they had gone a mile, and he was so far back that Gustines had to move him up on the outside, then, with no room to come through, had to take him even wider. Sometimes in races there seem to be just too many horses to pass or come through, and there are times when people like to say the jockey rode the hair off the horse. The Woodward was one of those races. The stretch-run and the finish were hair-raisers, with *Forego* charging up to win by a neck over *Arbees Boy* and *Group Plan*, who was a good third.

After making another one of his seven-furlong sprint appearances in October in the Vosburgh Handicap, where he carried 131 pounds and won smartly, *Forego* started in the two-mile Jockey Club Gold Cup on November 9th at Aqueduct. By the time the eight-horse field had gone a mile Gustines had him moving well out from the rail. He caught *Group Plan* before the quarter pole and simply drew away. *Copte*, the French invader from Longchamp, finished second, a badly tiring *Group Plan* finished third, and *Arbees Boy* was fourth. All four of them carried equal weight of 124 pounds. It was a brilliant end to the season. *Forego* was clearly the champion, the Horse of the Year for 1974. He was an older star than *Secretariat*, but he was a great star with much more to do.

As a five-year-old he started again down in Florida, carrying 129 pounds in the nine-furlong Seminole Handicap and winning going away. Two weeks later he won the Widner with 131 pounds, a record high weight for the race. There was no doubt that *Forego* truly loved Florida. The winter sunshine did him good and he seemed to mature more at five, if that could be possible. His big summer objective was again the rich but difficult New York handicap series.

He tuned up once more in the Carter at Aqueduct in a terrific rehearsal that saw him carry 134 pounds to victory, running the seven furlongs in 1:21-3/5. In the Metropolitan Mile, now at Aqueduct, he was assigned 136 pounds. The race was a sizzler, with the first six furlongs in 1:08-4/5 and the mile in 1:33-3/5. But the big weight was too much. After a long drive he finished third, less than a length behind *Gold and Myrrh* with 121 pounds and *Stop the Music* with 124.

On the Fourth of July he was back for the Brooklyn, this year at Belmont. He carried 132 pounds and never looked better. It was a familiar sight. He stayed back early, well out from the rail and possible traffic, then made a bold move on the turn and followed up with a stretch-run that had that championship quality to it. He gave *Monetary Principal* 23 pounds and drew off by a length and a half. Gustines was never really worried. The time of 1:54-4/5 was a new track record for the mile and a quarter.

While the Brooklyn win duplicated his feat in 1974, in the Suburban he improved on his previous year's performance. At the end of the new Suburban distance of a mile and a half, *Forego* was the winner by a head over his old rival *Arbees Boy*. He carried 134 pounds, *Arbees Boy* 118. It was a remarkable performance that gave *Forego* a score of two out of three in the big summer handicaps.

Now came the challenge to match his two-out-of-three record in the fall series, again on familiar Belmont ground. As a prelude, he started on September 1st in the Governor Stakes at nine furlongs and met some new competition. A top field of ten went to the post, including *Forego* the highweight at 134 pounds, *Ancient Title* with 130, *Foolish Pleasure* at 125, *Wajima* at 115, down to *Media* and *American History* with 111 each. Braulio Baeza rode a great race on *Wajima* and beat out *Foolish Pleasure* with Angel Cordero by a head. Two lengths back in third was *Ancient Title* with Sandy Hawley, while *Forego* with Gustines came along with a mild rally for fourth.

He met *Wajima* again in the Marlboro Cup. With 129 pounds, *Forego* came through on the inside and got to the front, but *Wajima* with only 119 took him on. It was an outstanding horserace, run in 2:00 flat for the ten furlongs, 1/5 off the record. The winning margin was only a head, but *Wajima* won in the end. *Ancient Title* was a distant third. It was still an improvement on his third-place finish in the Marlboro in 1974, and there were still two more races to go.

But, unfortunately, the Woodward Stakes on September 27th was his final race for the season. It was a six-horse race with the Belmont Stakes winner *Avatar* in the field, as well as *Wajima*, as sharp as he had ever been. Not surprisingly, these two were away on top, but to the complete surprise of nearly everyone *Forego* was right there with them. The new early pace tactics placed him on the outside of the two leaders around the first turn and down the backstretch to the far turn. Gustines let him run and at the three-eighths pole *Forego* and *Wajima* started to race all-out. Head to head they stayed locked together until the final sixteenth when *Forego* drew away to win by a length and three-quarters. The huge Belmont crowd cheered him the way they used to cheer *Kelso* in the sixties.

He was set to go after the two-mile Jockey Club Gold Cup that he had won so powerfully the year before, but just two days before the race he pulled the suspensory of his left foreleg and the leg filled. He was blistered and sent for an extended rest on John Ward's farm in Lexington, Kentucky. The great *Forego* was temporarily closed for repairs. In 1975, he had won six out of nine races, finishing second in one, third in one, and out of the money in one. His victories had been from seven furlongs to a mile and a half, and he had carried over 130 pounds in every winning race but one. His earnings for the year totalled $429,521.

While *Forego*'s retirement was only temporary, his wonderfully understanding trainer Sherrill Ward had to step down for good, for he suffered terribly from an osteo-arthritic condition of the hip. Ward left behind a prediction that *Forego* would do even better in 1976 because, as he said, the big horse was only now approaching peak development. Martha Gerry announced that Frank Whiteley and his son David would take over the training of her Lazy F Ranch horses. *Forego* was shipped down to Whiteley in Camden, South Carolina.

Under Whiteley's expertise, he raced eight times as a six-year-old. He trained lightly until April, then headed north to New York. This was a departure from the usual pattern, the first time *Forego* had missed his beloved Florida sun. His objectives were the ever-familiar New York summer series of rich historic handicaps, then, if all went well, the big ones again in the fall.

He carried 126 pounds just once during the year, and that was in his first start on May 20th at Belmont. The race was a seven-furlong sprint and *Forego* came home the winner in 1:22 flat. On May 31st he carried 130 pounds to a win in the one-mile Metropolitan, and followed up with a win with Jacinto Vasquez in the nine-furlong Nassau County, carrying 132 pounds. Gustines was back for the Suburban on July 5th over yet another new distance of one mile and three-sixteenths, and, with 134 pounds on him, *Forego* missed winning by a nose to *Foolish Pleasure*.

The Suburban was a heart-breaker, but he came right back and won in the ten-furlong Brooklyn, again with 134 pounds. The Brooklyn win, his third in a row, was achieved in classic *Forego* style. He was unhurried early, took some considerable bumping, raced widest of all, then galloped down the stretch for a strong finish that saw him going away from both *Lord Rebeau* and *Foolish Pleasure*. The scene in Aqueduct's winner's circle was historic; it was the last time that *Forego* and Gustines were together. They had proved to be a magnificent combination, winning twenty-two of their thirty-three races.

After Jacinto Vasquez rode *Forego* to a third-place finish in the Amory L. Haskell Handicap at beautiful Monmouth Park in Oceanport, New Jersey, the world's winningest jockey, Bill Shoemaker, got the mount on *Forego* for the nine-furlong Woodward. *Forego* had won the last two runnings carrying 126 pounds in the weight-for-age stake, but now the Woodward was a handicap. *Forego*'s greatness was penalized by 135 pounds. Shoemaker let him break slowly, did not hurry him, saved ground all the way to the three-furlong pole, then came

out for his move. He won going away from *Dance Spell* and *Honest Pleasure* in a very fast 1:45-4/5, only 2/5 off *Secretariat*'s American record for the distance.

The Woodward triumph left no doubt that *Forego* would be named champion again. But, just to be sure, he came back for an encore and ran the finest race of his career. In the Marlboro Cup Handicap on October 2nd, the Belmont track was sloppy. Eleven horses started from the gate. *Honest Pleasure* went right to the front, full of run and relishing the going. Racing well out from the rail, he actually opened up his lead coming into the stretch. *Father Hogan* tested him strongly, but *Honest Pleasure* was running the race of his life; he kept on going. *Forego*, who had broken well at the start, was saved for a big rush on the next turn for home. Impossible as it seemed *Forego* started moving, as usual on the outside. *Honest Pleasure* seemed invincible, especially with the sloppy going, but *Forego* ran as if possessed. In the final yards he got up to win by a head in one of the boldest and most courageous stretch-runs ever seen. Shoemaker was thrilled and declared that *Forego* was the best he had ever ridden. Sherrill Ward's prediction had been unbelievably accurate. *Forego* at six had won six of eight races, with one second and one third, and had earned $491,701.

Whiteley brought him back seven more times as a seven-year-old, with 'The Shoe' in the saddle for every race. He followed the previous year's program, starting out with a winning run in a sprint, then going up against the track handicapper. The lowest weight he carried all season was 133 pounds. He won the Metropolitan with 133, the Nassau County with a huge 136, finished second by a neck with 138 pounds in the mile and a quarter Suburban, and lost the Brooklyn at a mile and a half by eleven lengths to *Great Contractor*, but still managed to be second with 137 pounds up.

On August 6th, for the first and only time, he raced at Saratoga. The race was the Whitney and the track was sloppy. *Forego* carried 136 pounds and finished last. But he went back to New York and Belmont Park and carried 133 pounds to win the Woodward again. It was his last race of the year, because the same old leg began bothering him again. In seven starts, he had won four, been second in two and and been unplaced in one. He had earned $268,740.

Forego actually came back at eight to end his great career. In June he won a four-horse Allowance Race at seven furlongs, then went into the Suburban on the Fourth of July. The track was sloppy for the ten-furlong race, and *Forego* went off at 9–10. He was beaten by fourteen lengths and finished fifth. It was the 57th and final race of an incredible campaign, a campaign that was hard-fought, with the inevitable wear and tear of racing that the great champions, particularly, know and must endure.

The history of American racing is rich in the stories of great geldings and their long years of racing. Two of them, *Exterminator* and *Kelso*, have already been honoured by induction into the Hall of Fame. *Forego*'s great achievements in the seventies almost certainly entitle him to the same honour.

Today he runs in his paddock at John Ward's training centre in Lexington, Kentucky. He still runs hard when he hears and then sees the fields of horses racing down the backstretch of neighbouring Keeneland Racetrack, but the steadiness in the old legs is gone. Gone, too, but not forgotten, are the great runs in the Metropolitan, the Suburban, the Brooklyn, the Widner, the Woodward, the Marlboro and the Jockey Club Gold Cup. These are the toughest races in America, but none of them were too tough for *Forego*.

Grundy

He had a look of eagles". The saying is as old as racing itself and means that the horse in question is one of rare quality, with the strength and speed of a champion. Though little heard in the world of racing since Irish actor Barry Fitzgerald immortalized the phrase while playing the wise old trainer in 'The Story of Seabiscuit', they were the only words that Peter Walwyn, England's leading trainer of 1974-75, could summon to express an all-important first impression that would never go away. Oddly enough, Walwyn's delivery was better than Fitzgerald's.

The horse that drew the response from Walwyn was a yearling colt from the Overbury Stud. Consigned to the 1973 sale, the colt boasted, at best, what discreet and kind people would call "interesting" breeding. His sire was *Great Nephew*, a horse with ability up to a mile and a quarter and a sire of some useful runners, but certainly of no big names. His dam was *Word From Lundy*, who won at distances up to two miles. Her staying ability came from her sire *Worden II*, who was good enough to win the second running of the Washington, D.C. International at Laurel, Maryland in 1953. *Word From Lundy*'s first foal was *Whirlow Green*, a fair handicap horse with ability up to nine furlongs. The colt that caught Walwyn's fancy was her second foal.

Breeding, the bloodlines, always fascinate, as do the actual accomplishments of the horses themselves. But it is the individual that must be scrutinized, because it is in the individual that greatness lies. It's just that sometimes it is so hard to see. Walwyn's first impressions included a reluctance to respond to the Overbury colt's colour. He though it unfashionable, rather washy for a chestnut. There was also the flaxen mane and tail that didn't seem

impressive. Yet there was something about him. "He had a look of eagles".

When the colt passed through the sales ring after being knocked down for 11,000 guineas, many observers simply dismissed him as another horse that was rather well-sold. For most, he was that flashy type of chestnut that never lives up to expectations, a weak sort when compared with a bay, at least on the average. But Peter Walwyn, bloodstock agent Keith Freeman, and Dr. Carlo Vittadini, who had become the adventuresome new owner, liked what others did not. They were overjoyed with their unique looking bargain, for that's what he proved to be—a very rare bargain indeed.

He was named *Grundy* and soon developed into what Walwyn called a tremendous character. He was alert and observant, very boisterous and always full of run, too much, in fact, in his canters. He needed two months to break in instead of the usual one, but it was all well worth it. He was a well-made colt, deep through the chest, and looked smaller than he really was. With time he developed into a very beautiful looking individual, with his flaxen mane and tail and fine arab head setting off his well-proportioned chestnut body. Best of all, he was sound and had 'legs like iron'. His action was faultless, and he learned to respond to riders of great strength, particularly Pat Eddery, England's new champion jockey.

Grundy and Eddery made their first start at Ascot in the six-furlong Granville Stakes on July 26, 1974. The going was good for the field of newcomers, and off his good training *Grundy* was made the second choice at 5–1. Eddery kept him close up behind the leaders until just before the final furlong, then he moved him over to the rails. A narrow opening was soon filled as *Grundy* and

Eddery squeezed through to win going away by two lengths. Their running mate *No Alimony* finished second, and the favourite *Amerrico* was third. It was a more than satisfying performance for the trio who now had a two-year-old colt that trained very well and raced very well, one that had speed to be well placed, maneuverability for his rider to use when needed, courage to race on even through the tightest of quarters, then additional speed to be clear at the end.

On August 30th they were at Kempton Park for the Sirenia Plate, another six-furlong effort. The going was firm for the nine-runner race, and halfway home there was *Grundy* making it all look very easy. He won by two and a half lengths. Immediately behind him were *Prospect Rainbow* and *Gisela*, and in fifth place, six lengths back, was *Sweet Reclaim*. This made *Grundy*'s win all the more impressive, because both *Prospect Rainbow* and *Sweet Reclaim* were fairly good two-year-olds who were generating some excitement. And they lived up to their notices, too, except where *Grundy* was concerned, *Prospect Rainbow* before Kempton and *Sweet Reclaim* after.

On September 11th at Doncaster, *Grundy* ran in the seven-furlong Champagne Stakes. Among the eight other runners were many of Britain's most promising two-year-olds, including *Whip It Quick*, the Coventry Stakes winner, and *Bold Pirate*, the runner-up in the Richmond Stakes at Goodwood. *Grundy* went off as the 8–5 favourite and at the halfway mark frightened his backers with a second-to-last position, made all the more precarious by heavy traffic everywhere that Eddery could see. As always, the alternatives of going through or going around posed plenty of risks. Narrow openings often close quickly, causing the advancing horse to take up, losing vital momentum, while end-runs often result in too much ground having to be covered. Coming to the final furlong, Eddery had no choice but to move *Grundy* over to the left. Once there he accelerated smoothly to join *Whip It Quick* and *Bold Pirate*. Needing only a few strides to put the race away, at the finish it was *Grundy* first by a half a length over *Whip It Quick*, with *Bold Pirate* third.

Grundy faced a new challenge on October 18th in Newmarket's William Hill Dewhurst Stakes. The ground was very soft and the distance was seven furlongs, conditions that go against speed and favour stamina. It would be a severe test for any two-year-old, but *Grundy*, who had shown all kinds of speed, now showed great amounts of stamina. He led the final quarter of a mile and won by six lengths over *Steel Heart*, with *Baldur* finishing third. The Dewhurst was the fourth and final start of his two-year-old year in 1974 and, along with the Champagne

result, clearly demonstrated that *Grundy* was Britain's undisputed two-year-old champion, as well as the favourite for the first jewel in England's Triple Crown, the Two Thousand Guineas at Newmarket.

Grundy progressed very well through the winter, but then suffered a most peculiar and quite awful accident in March. He was kicked in the face by a stable companion. With the honeycomb of facial bones fractured, his training was interrupted. The interruption was long enough for him to lose essential conditioning, for on April 19, 1975 *Grundy* went down to his first defeat in his initial start at three. He wasn't disgraced, however, because he managed a second to *Mark Anthony* over Newbury's seven furlongs of very heavy ground. He had had the lead, but weakened and lost by two lengths. The race, the Greenham Stakes, was his only prep for the big Classic at Newmarket on May 3rd.

The Two Thousand Guineas, at one mile, seemed ideal for *Grundy*. Two furlongs from home he was in the lead. Then along came *Bolkonski*, who had been one of the best Italian two-year-olds of 1974. *Grundy* responded gamely to Eddery's strong urging, but it wasn't enough to catch *Bolkonski*, who won by half a length.

There were now some doubts about *Grundy*'s chances in the Derby, but when Peter Walwyn shipped him to the Curragh for the Irish Two Thousand Guineas on May 17th, *Grundy* left no doubt about his sharpness and speed. The ground was good in this one-mile Classic, but the pace was rather slow. Three furlongs from home, *Grundy* was 'crying to run'. He simply pulled himself to the front, held off his nearest rival, *Monsanto*, and won easily by a length and a half. His Newbury conqueror *Mark Anthony* was third.

Grundy went in as the 7–2 choice for the Derby Stakes at Epsom on June 4th. He faced eighteen runners, many of whom were thought to be strong challengers. One of these was *Green Dancer*, the best from France and a son of *Nijinsky II*. His credentials were certainly impressive, for he had lost only once and had raced so strongly in the Poule d'Essai des Poulains and the Prix Lupin that the French thought him their best challenger in many years.

The going was good on this most wonderful of racing days, and the running was the third fastest since the war. *Grundy* settled down very well for the early part and gave Eddery no problems whatsoever. He maintained such a good position that when he reached Tattenham Corner he was fourth, with fourteen runners behind him. He responded to Eddery's uring in the straight as if he had been in mile and a half affairs all his life. *Anne's Pretender* was a very strong galloper, but not strong enough. *Grundy* caught him and widened on his field to win by three of the easiest lengths seen in years. The fine filly *Nobiliary* was second, and *Hunza Dancer* third, both of them in the frame with strong finishes. *Green Dancer* was beaten by ten lengths and won a place in history as one more top choice who failed when it counted most. He went home to France with many of his supporters far from speechless, but certainly not too coherent.

After *Grundy*'s Derby triumph, it was announced that the Levy Board had acquired a three-quarter share in him for three-quarters of a million pounds. His future as a sire at the National Stud at Newmarket was secure, but there were conditions to the deal: he would not race in the Prix de l'Arc de Triomphe at Longchamp, nor would he race as a four-year-old. These strictures were understandable, but not tolerable to the public, for no one ever wants to see a Derby winner, and a most impressive one at that, put away after such a brief career. But the furor abated as *Grundy* went out in glory.

One June 28th he returned to Ireland for the Irish Sweeps Derby at the Curragh. He was just below even in the great mile and a half Classic and gave his backers a wonderful run. His chief rival was *King Pellinore*, a strong second choice who later made a name for himself in the rich races for older horses in California. *Grundy* gave Eddery a good trip and won in hand after what was now his usual strong bid. *King Pellinore* was second, and *Anne's Pretender* came third.

A month later, on July 26th, *Grundy* was tested against older horses in the King George VI and Queen Elizabeth Diamond Stakes. It was one of those beautiful, clear English summer days when all seems right with the world. *Grundy* made the day memorable. Among the eleven runners preparing to go the mile and half were *Dahlia*, back after winning the King George VI two years in a row, and three horses that Major Dick Hern sent out: *Highest*, a good miler for pace; *Kinglet*, a good stayer for late strength; and *Bustino*, Hern's best for the finish. Any of the three were capable of winning.

The pacemakers worked Hern's plan to perfection until it was time for *Bustino* to come on. With half a mile to go, *Grundy* picked up speed as soon as *Bustino* got the lead. There were four lengths to make up going into the straight, and the thought occurred to Eddery that the task was so formidable the worst just might happen. *Bustino* was setting an incredible pace, and whenever it seemed like *Grundy* would get him, he would find a little more. Inside the last furlong, both horses were flat-out, but *Grundy* prevailed and crossed the finish half a length in front. It was an all-out effort, and when they came back to the thousands of cheers and tears awaiting them both horses were exhausted. It was a magnificent race on a splendid day with two of England's best.

It should have ended there with dignity and a flourish, but, unfortunately, *Grundy* went to York for the Benson and Hedges Gold Cup. He finished fourth, eleven lengths down the course to *Dahlia*, *Card King* and *Star Appeal*. It was a sad ending to a glorious summer of success.

Grundy was champion three-year-old of Britain, and was syndicated for an estimated $2,000,000. He won eight of his eleven starts, and earned £326,421 before starting his new career as a sire at the National Stud where he is today. He is now the handsome chestnut stallion with the flaxen mane and tail who won two Derbies and who, in the King George VI, ran as great a race as anyone had ever seen. The look of eagles is still there, too, but more people than Peter Walwyn can see it now.

Mill Reef

The first thing that struck trainer Ian Balding about *Mill Reef* was that he seemed small in stature, but full of quality. In training he was never bigger than fifteen hands, three inches, though, surprisingly, he grew more after his racing was over. His head and hocks were small, but perfectly proportioned. His coat was Balding's favourite colour, a dark bay brown that was always the first to come in in the spring. He had perfect balance; Balding said he never saw him stumble or slip or take a false stride, something most horses usually manage to do. He also had perfect action, the best Balding had ever seen, and was able to handle any kind of going. In his races he could manage terrific speed early on and maintain it over distance, or do the opposite and settle easily in the early running then accelerate when required. He was an outstanding, even brilliant two-year-old, and a marvellous horse for the long three-year-old Classics. He had natural speed, stamina, the talent of a great horse, intelligence, a very good temperament, and one extra quality that trainers rejoice in—he was very easy to train. He was the perfect horse who's life on the racecourse came to an abrupt and near-tragic end.

Mill Reef was by *Never Bend* from the *Princequillo* mare *Milan Mill*. He was bred at Paul Mellon's estate in Virginia, but had his career on the other side of the Atlantic. In racing he never knew the feeling of dirt breaking from under him, only the give of grass, the beautiful looking grass found on English racecourses like Salisbury, where many people say they have the finest grass in England.

It was there on May 30, 1970 that he made his first start in a program of two-year-old races that Ian Balding had thought out for this promising little colt. The race was a five-furlong sprint. There is no better test this early in the season than the straight mile of the Salisbury course.

It's all rising ground from the start to the finish, except for the dip four and a half furlongs from home. Some jockeys prefer to bring their horses over to the stand side for the better ground, but not all of them. Sometimes a race will divide into two groups and the course announcer will describe the running order on the stand side, followed by the order on the far side. It didn't matter much to jockey Geoff Lewis where he was with *Mill Reef*. He was never headed. He led his field of eleven all the way and won by four lengths.

Mill Reef and Lewis made an impressive repeat performance in the Coventry Stakes at Royal Ascot, Britain's premiere racecourse in the beautiful Berkshires, where *Mill Reef* did exactly as Lewis pleased. He made all the running and won in a canter by eight lengths. They then crossed the Channel to Maisons-Laffitte for one of French racing's top two-year-old stakes, the Prix Robert Papin. One of the nine runners in the five and a half-furlong race was *My Swallow*, the champion juvenile of France, who went in as the favourite and justified the role by winning, but only by a head. *Mill Reef* was a strong second in a game finish after making a good rally. *My Swallow* never lost that year, winning all seven of his starts, including the four biggest races for two-year-olds on the French calendar.

The narrow loss didn't detract from the interest *Mill Reef* was arousing, interest that was heightened further by his start on August 20th in the historic Gimcrack Stakes at York. The going was soft for the six-furlong stake, but *Mill Reef* loved it. In an astonishing display he seemed to cry out, 'Let me run'. And that was what he did, going to the front under a hold with two furlongs to go, then cantering right away with Lewis sitting still to win by ten lengths. *Green God*, *Grand Chaudiere* and five others were up the track. There wasn't a two-year-old race in England to come close to *Mill Reef*'s Gimcrack, and his brilliance was now more than apparent. People were becoming excited.

One month later he was out at Kempton for the six-furlong Imperial Stakes. Lewis kept him from being an early leader, then had to make him run with a quarter of a mile to go. It was not easy, there was no doubt of that, but there was no doubt either about the finish. *Mill Reef* won by a length, with *Hecla* second and *Gertie Millar* third. It was his toughest win of the year.

He finished the season by winning the important seven-furlong Dewhurst Stakes at Newmarket by four lengths over *Wenceslas* and *Lombardo*. The *Mill Reef* run now seemed familiar. He would wait until the final two furlongs, then he would simply pull away, producing that extra speed just when Lewis wanted. Balding had him trained to perfection.

His debut year had been a very good year, and nearly everything that one could think of suggested that *Mill Reef* would be even better at three. Everything, that is, except his *Never Bend* breeding. The British in the early seventies still had not seen enough of the splendid North American individuals to realize that the clues to their futures were best found in their races, rather than in their pedigrees. Their races clearly showed their tremendous ability to accelerate boldly, their courage when hard-pressed, and their ability to be perfectly trained. They could conserve their speed until needed. A plodder hasn't got any speed and so can run all night, but a horse like *Mill Reef* with great natural speed that can be contained, saved and then used, can run all night too. He can just do it faster.

At three, *Mill Reef* started to run all day, opening the 1971 season in April at Newbury in the seven-furlong Greenham Stakes. He won by four lengths, beating *Breeders Dream* and *Swing Easy*, then went on to one of the world's most famous races at a flat mile, the Two Thousand Guineas Stakes run each year at Newmarket since 1809.

The race, over the straight Rowley Mile Course, is the highlight of the Spring meet. Only six horses went to the post on May 1st, not because of any shortage, but more because half the field looked impossible to beat. *My Swallow* was undefeated in eight starts, one of which was a prep for the Guineas, *Brigadier Gerard* was also undefeated, having won four for four, though he had not yet started in 1971, and *Mill Reef* was six for seven, having just failed to catch *My Swallow* in their only other meeting at two. At the start *My Swallow* went to the front and led for three-quarters of a mile. *Mill Reef* pursued him and got the lead on the hill, but he couldn't hold it for long. *Brigadier Gerard* was too strong and too good, and moved past *Mill Reef* to win by three lengths. *My Swallow* finished third. The Guineas proved that *Brigadier Gerard* was probably the best miler in a long, long time. *Mill Reef* had simply met his match at that distance. It was to be his last defeat.

For the 1971 Derby Stakes on June 2nd, twenty-one runners took to the field. *Mill Reef* turned out for it in great style. His action on the way down to the start was so impressive that the punters were greatly inspired, for he was a more than generous 3–1. For the first part of the race, Lewis was content to let him run along about fifth. As they started down the hill he lost position a bit, until Lewis asked him to keep up. He responded without expending very much and arrived in fourth place at Tattenham corner for the turn into the straight. *Linden Tree*, *Lombardo* and *Homeric* were in front, and all were driving full out. A furlong further, *Linden Tree* still led. The others were tiring, but not *Mill Reef* who started coming full of run. It was too much for *Linden Tree* to hold off *Mill Reef* after surviving earlier challenges. He tried hard, but simply could not do it. *Mill Reef* was the stronger and would not be denied the lead which he held right to the wire to win by two lengths.

While *Mill Reef* had shown that there were few other three-year-olds who could match his speed, he had not yet been tested against older horses. His first such test came about a month after the Derby in Sandown's ten-furlong Eclipse Stakes. There were six runners, one of them the very sharp and classy French four-year-old grey *Caro*. The year before in the French Derby, *Caro* had been very close to *Sassafras*, the horse that broke *Nijinsky II*'s undefeated record in the Arc. As an older horse in 1971 *Caro* was undefeated, with victories in the Prix d'Harcourt, the Prix Ganay and the Prix Dollar, the first two at ten-furlongs.

In the Eclipse *Welsh Pageant* went away fast and set the pace until *Bright Beam* put him away. *Quebracho* then took over second from a tiring *Welsh Pageant*. *Mill Reef* and Geoff Lewis were biding their time in fourth, while *Caro* and Maurice Philliperon stalked them most carefully. *Quayside* was no threat at all. Suddenly, Lewis asked *Mill Reef* to move, and just as he did so the pace-setters had had enough. With two tiring Sandown furlongs to go, he went to the front in a dazzling move that prompted Philliperon to ask *Caro* for everything. The effort was enough to get *Caro* to *Mill Reef*, but for no more than a sixteenth of a mile. Then the *Caro* move was over, almost as quickly as it had started, while *Mill Reef* continued to pick up speed, running so fast that he crossed the finish four lengths ahead of *Caro*.

The Eclipse was another terrific performance by both horse and jockey, and also a great training feat for Ian Balding, who used the race as a prep for the King George VI and Queen Elizabeth Stakes at Ascot on July 24th.

The Ascot middle distance Classic drew a star-studded field headed by the English Derby winner, *Mill Reef*, the Irish Derby winner, *Irish Ball*, and the Italian Derby winner, *Ortis*. Also in the field were *Stintino*, third to *Nijinsky* II the year before, and six others who had managed in-the-money finishes in the Classics. Little *Mill Reef*, compact and strong looking, wasn't the number one eye-catcher in the paddock, but he made up for that by going down for the start in rare form. Once the race was on he was more than impressive, especially when he rounded the turn in third position behind *Ortis* and *Poletico*. Once in the straight, he quickened his pace and advanced to the front just as Lewis asked him. An eighth of a mile from the finish he made it no contest as he gained more strength with every stride. He hit the wire six lengths in front for an easy win over some very talented horses. *Ortis* was second, *Acclimatization* third.

There could be only one encore to such a magnificent run, a start in the only mile and a half Classic ranking even ahead of the King George VI, the Prix de l'Arc de Triomphe. The British love these cross-Channel invasions, especially when they feel they have got the best horse. The year before they had faithfully backed *Nijinsky* II and Lester Piggott, only to have the French Derby winner *Sassafras* and Yves Saint-Martin beat them out by a neck. But *Mill Reef* and Geoff Lewis made no mistakes, living up to their notices and winning the Arc in a most impressive fashion. *Pistol Packer* was second and *Cambrizzia* third, while *Caro* finished fourth.

Mill Reef's Arc win at 7–10 odds was accomplished with the same strategy seen before, the best strategy for the Paris race. The forwardly-placed runners usually do the best, and it's also an advantage if ground can be saved. *Mill Reef* found much of the Arc made to order for his style of running. Lewis had him in the right places at all the right times, so when they came into the straight for the short run to the wire *Mill Reef* was well positioned in the first group. He had to come off the rails once when straightened out, but Lewis quickly got him back. Then he turned on the acceleration. In the last furlong he drew clear and won by three lengths. Fittingly, he was named England's Horse of the Year for 1971.

Mill Reef was clearly an outstanding prospect for racing at four, and he lived up to expectations by winning Longchamp's Prix Ganay by ten lengths in April and Epsom's Coronation Cup Derby week by a neck. Sadly, they were his last two starts. First a virus infection that plagued Balding's yard at Kingsclere kept him away from the summer races. He managed to recover from the infection, but while preparing for the Cumberland Lodge Stakes, a prelude to another try at the Arc, he broke his near-foreleg, shattering the lower two and a half inches of the cannon bone as well as the inner sesamoid, and damaging the rim of the pastern bone.

In earlier years, such an accident invariably would have been fatal, but new techniques had been developed and had been used in the U.S. with great success to save the life of *Hoist The Flag*. The surgical procedures in themselves were not dangerous, but there was always the possibility that the horse would thrash around so violently on coming out of the anaesthetic that the painstaking labours of the veterinary surgeons would all have been for nothing. Preparation proved to be the key for the first attempt in England to use the new techniques.

An old chapel in Ian Balding's yard was converted into a temporary equine hospital. For a week, while veterinarians were rounded up in the U.S., Britain and Europe, a sedated *Mill Reef* became familiar with his new surroundings. His people continued their normal daily routines. These precautions resulted in perfect preparation. So relaxed was *Mill Reef* during surgery that to the complete astonishment of his team of three veterinarians he needed only half the anaesthetic usual in such cases. He was never in a state of anxiety, sensing that everything would be all right. Over six long hours a special stainless steel compression plate was inserted, then held by three screws which pinned the broken pieces to the cannon bone. The damage to the sesamoid bone and the rim of the pastern healed perfectly without surgery. He wore a plaster cast for six weeks, then a felt support for two.

He was placed in a special recovery stall where the walls were lined with bales of hay. There remained concern that when he wanted to lie down he could do himself great harm, but *Mill Reef* managed everything wonderfully. Balding wondered just how he was managing so well and set up a careful watch which revealed *Mill Reef*'s method. He would lean his body against the wall of hay bales, then, with some of the weight off his feet, he would carefully slide himself down. He recovered beautifully and through patient handling and care he soon regained his confidence.

Syndicated for $5,000,000, *Mill Reef* is now the star

stallion of the National Stud at Newmarket and one of Britain's leading sires. Before his time it was not unusual for many horses who thrilled British racegoers to be exported when their racing was done; most of his American-bred contemporaries returned to their native land. But *Mill Reef* stayed and started a trend toward stopping the best from getting away, especially the Derby winners. *Grundy, Troy* and *Shirley Heights*, *Mill Reef's* greatest son who won the Derby Stakes for Lord Halifax in 1978, have all remained in Britain and have done their part to improve the bloodstock and thereby maintain the best traditions of British racing and breeding.

Mill Reef's contributions, past and future, to these traditions are already legend. He won twelve of his fourteen races and earned £301,218. He won many of those races in such a brilliant manner that there is no question he deserves a high place in racing's annals. Undoubtedly one of the most remarkable thoroughbreds of the seventies, many would proclaim him the best since *Sea-Bird* and *Ribot*, one of the greatest of the century.

The Minstrel

Victoria Park, Northern Dancer and *Cool Reception* put Canada on the racing map in the sixties, running against the very best in American racing. *Victoria Park* was the first in 1960 with his good third in the Kentucky Derby and his second in the Preakness. In 1964, *Northern Dancer*, as nearly everyone now knows, was the first Canadian-bred to win the Kentucky Derby and the Preakness, while missing the Triple Crown with a third in the Belmont. Then in 1967, *Cool Reception* raced the Derby winner *Proud Clarion* into defeat in the Belmont Stakes. Tragically, one-eighth of a mile from the finish his leg snapped, and it was only momentum that carried him through the next twelve seconds to finish a gallant second to *Damascus*. The fatal injury robbed Canadian breeding of a potentially great sire.

All three of these horses were bred by E.P. Taylor, now the world's leading thoroughbred breeder, at his famous Windfields Farm. After carrying Taylor's turquoise and gold colours in triumph to the American tracks, both *Victoria Park* and *Northern Dancer* were retired to Taylor's farms for breeding. *Victoria Park* is still standing at stud at his vast Oshawa, Ontario farm, while *Northern Dancer* is another Canadian under the roof at Windfields' Maryland farm in Chesapeake City.

Both stallions are getting on now, but both have already more than paid their way. *Victoria Park* has sired three Queen's Plate winners, *Almoner, Victoria Song* and *Kennedy Road*, and gained a good reputation as a sire to watch because of his fillies like *Victorian Queen*. *Northern Dancer* has sired more than five dozen stakes winners, including the great *Nijinsky II*, the first horse to win an English Triple Crown in thirty-five years. Theoretically, a share of the stallion should sell for $200,000 a service

with no guarantee of a live foal, but the shares are not for sale.

The *Northern Dancers* are always at a premium, with his yearlings automatically commanding six figures wherever they're sold. One such yearling was a bay colt of *Northern Dancer*'s from a *Victoria Park* mare named *Fleur*. He sold for $250,000 and ran in France under the name of *Far North*. Taylor tried the same combination again, and in 1974 he got a flashy looking chestnut colt complete with white all over his face and four white feet.

The colt's appearance likely made some prospective buyers uneasy, for there are old sayings still current in the racing world that often give some people pause. One maintains that "Too much white hair means there's a weakness somewhere". Another goes, "One white foot, buy a horse; two white feet, try a horse; three white feet, look well about him; four white feet, do without him". This old adage comes out of the traditional good foot guide and seems to plague many people who, at times, probably wished they had known better. There were even those who doubted *Secretariat*'s ability because of his three white feet.

But a syndicate that included Ireland's Vincent O'Brien and Britain's Robert Sangster obviously didn't believe in the old sayings, because they bought *Far North*'s full brother for $200,000. They probably thought, and rightly so, that a good horse makes any colour look good. They named their horse *The Minstrel*.

As a two-year-old in 1976, *The Minstrel* made only three starts, two in Ireland in September and one in England in October. He was in the hands of the great Irish trainer Vincent O'Brien who used a six-furlong sprint in the May Stakes at the Curragh for the debut. *The Minstrel*, with Thomas Murphy up, was the favourite and won by five lengths. *Mississippi* was second, twelve lengths to the good of the third horse *Toomai*. It was a twelve-runner race and *The Minstrel* made a shambles of it.

His next start was on September 25th at Leopardstown, this time at seven furlongs. Lester Piggott had the mount and he was careful with *The Minstrel*, letting him settle down until the last part of the race when he went away to win by a length. When it comes to O'Brien's two-year-olds, the switch to Piggott has often proved an indication of quality, and this time was no exception.

The Minstrel was shipped to England for his final start of the year on October 15th in Newmarket's big two-year-old classic, the seven-furlong William Hill Dewhurst Stakes. There was a good deal of excitement about this race, because in recent years *Nijinksy II*, *Mill Reef* and *Grundy* had all won the Dewhurst at two, then gone on to take the Derby at three. With Piggott on him again, *The Minstrel* went in as the favourite. At the start he ran eleventh in the eleven-runner field. *Saros*, ridden by Pat Eddery, and the second-choice favourite off an easy win at Goodwood, was in the lead. At the five-furlong marker *The Minstrel* made a smart move from the rear and was on his way, racing away from *Saros* in the last quarter to win without being driven by four lengths.

The speculation about *The Minstrel* now began in earnest. For those going to his familiar Canadian pedigree, however, there was a trap. *Northern Dancer* had lost the Belmont Stakes at a mile and a half and, therefore, had not been what's called a true middle distance horse, or stayer. What has often been overlooked, however, is that he was a horse with great natural speed and acceleration and that in the Belmont he raced along under 'double wraps', finally giving up after 'crying to run'. It is true that he sired very good ten-furlong runners, but it is also true that he sired *Nijinsky II*. People used to talk about *Nijinsky II* not being a stayer because of his breeding, at least until the 1970 Derby.

As a wry old horseman once said, "They can't read their pedigrees". To find the answers to the three-year-old Classics, it is necessary to go back to the individual. And *The Minstrel* was a great individual, an extremely fast colt that had run on when asked. If a horse moves when his rider asks him to and accelerates with ease, if he has gameness, the ability to really run when pressed, then he's a very special kind of racehorse. "Never mind the ones that fold up like a two dollar suitcase as soon as someone looks them in the eye."

The doubts about *The Minstrel*'s staying power were not eased when he came along rather stubbornly at the

beginning of his three-year-old season. He was at Ascot on April 2nd for his first start in the Two Thousand Guineas Trial at seven furlongs. He won, beating *Gairloch*, but certainly not in any exciting manner. Even Lester Piggott must have wondered. There is no better judge of a horse's chances from one race to the next, and Piggott's only criterion for selecting his mount is, if possible, to be on the one with the best chance.

In his next start, the Two Thousand Guineas at Newmarket over the distance of one mile, *The Minstrel* simply was not good enough, finishing third behind *Nebbiolo* and *Tachypous*. He did beat *Gairloch* again, but that was hardly a great feat. Those who doubted the flashy chestnut's potential at three were now in their element. The one-mile Guineas, they conceded reluctantly, was the one Classic this 'speed-type' might win, and now he hadn't even managed that. The next big question for them was what would Lester do for the Derby? On May 13th *The Minstrel* was back in Ireland at the Curragh for his third race of the year, the Irish Two Thousand Guineas Stakes at a mile. Again he lost. *Pompapaul* beat him this time, and the question about Lester and what he would do became even more persistent.

Britain's champion jockey had won the Derby eight times. This year he seemed destined to ride a *Red God* colt called *Blushing Groom*. As a two-year-old, *Blushing Groom* had been the champion of his age in Europe, winning five of his six starts. He had raced past all of his opposition in French racing's four big tests for two-year-olds, convincing everyone of his potential when he beat England's champion *J.O. Tobin* in the Grand Criterium. So far as a three-year-old he had started in two one-mile races in France and had won them both. He had shown tremendous speed, but his connections needed more than easy miles; they needed tougher distances. He had missed the French Classic Trial, the Prix Lupin, but had raced in a morning trial instead. He had won it, beating as good a horse as *Exceller*, but *Exceller* had already proven that morning trials didn't interest him that much. *Blushing Groom*'s Epsom preparation began to look too light. Piggott certainly thought so, for he chose to ride *The Minstrel*.

Derby Day is a magnificent day, one of those wonderful, unforgettable English outings that begin with the traffic jams that seem to back up from the vast racecourse property all the way to Trafalgar Square, and end with a misplaced London street violinist playing 'Everything in Life is Beautiful'. The British say half a million people come to the downs just to be there, and it's easy to believe.

Twenty-two runners appeared in the saddling enclosure surrounded by the milling crowd. *The Minstrel* had gotten into a great lather at the Curragh with a huge crowd on hand and, with his memory of *Nijinsky II* getting quite washy in a similar situation before the Arc de Triomphe, Vincent O'Brien decided to take no chances at Epsom. He made sure that *The Minstrel* couldn't hear a thing by filling both of his ears with cotton wool.

Lester Piggott's strategy at Epsom has always fully utilized the particular talents of his mount, and there is no jockey anywhere in the world who knows this historic course the way he does. So, Piggott waited with *The Minstrel* during the early running. Then, just when he wanted to, he started after the leaders, always with much in reserve. When they reached the famous Tattenham Corner, *Milliondollarman* led from *Hot Grove*, with *The Minstrel* on the outside of the favourite *Caporello*. *Blushing Groom* was back a few more lengths. Into the straight, *Hot Grove* with Willie Carson came on to take the lead from *Milliondollarman*. Piggott then asked *The Minstrel* for that famous *Northern Dancer* acceleration that all his good 'natural speed horses' seem to have. The acceleration was there and it carried him forward up to *Hot Grove* for a long, furious battle that lasted a full quarter of a mile. Approaching the wire, it was *The Minstrel* on the outside of *Hot Grove*. *The Minstrel*'s head was right down, his ears were pinned, and Piggott was urging him right-handed for all he was worth. Carson tried his best, but it was just no use. *The Minstrel* won by a neck. It was a sensational performance by both horse and rider, and the first Derby win for Robert Sangster.

In the Irish Sweeps Derby on June 25th, they did it again, but not nearly so narrowly. They beat *Lucky Sovereign*, who had been unplaced at Epsom, by a length and a half, with *Classic Example* a neck behind in third. The Irish cheers were stilled when the Curragh stewards held an inquiry into the possibility of interference in the last furlong, but the objection was disallowed. *The Minstrel* had won his easiest race.

His hardest race came soon after in the King George VI and Queen Elizabeth Diamond Stakes at Ascot on July 23rd. This was his sixth start in almost twelve weeks and his third at a mile and a half, but there was now a major difference. He was in with the older horses in training, the best of Europe seeking a prize second only to Longchamp's Arc de Triomphe.

On King George Day *The Minstrel* looked splendid and showed once again that racing at Classic middle distances certainly agreed with him. He raced along on his own courage in the early running, and approaching the final turn he was sixth. Behind him was *Exceller*, the

American-bred who was France's best at the distance, *Crystal Palace*, the top French three-year-old, and *Crow*, a very good British horse. Ahead of him were two dangerous Classic runners from the older ranks, *Bruni* and *Orange Bay*.

Piggott sent him through a narrow opening, cleverly saving ground. Soon he was in front with a quarter of a mile to go. *Orange Bay* and Pat Eddery never let him get away, forcing him over every yard of ground and finally coming up on his inside with a final charge that seemed almost sure of victory. But *The Minstrel*, absolutely all-out, kept going. Both jockeys were at it right-handed, nonstop. Both horses, necks stretched, matched steps stride for stride. *The Minstrel*'s lead was slipping away; *Orange Bay* was getting to him. Somehow, *The Minstrel* managed to keep his head in front to hold the lead and win. *Exceller* with Freddy Head completed a tremendous run to get up for a fast-closing third. *The Minstrel*'s thrilling, desperate finish was reminiscent of his sire's performance in 1964 on the first Saturday in May, when *Northern Dancer* held off *Hill Rise*, held him even in fact, and showed the kind of speed a wild horse might have.

The King George VI victory marked the end of an all too short but tremendously exciting racing career for one of the finest horses Canada has ever produced. (During his time there was a tendency in Britain to refer to *The Minstrel* as an American horse, but that is like calling *Hyperion* French. He was as Canadian as *Northern Dancer*.) He won seven out of nine races over two seasons, earned $570,605, and was syndicated for $9,000,000. Now at stud at E.P. Taylor's Windfields Farm in Maryland, he shares the stallion barn with his illustrious sire.

Compact, racy, and above all strong, he remains a horse with terrific personality and a wonderful sense of fun that brings smiles and laughter from his handlers and visitors alike. A photographer assigned to a formal portrait session was recently the butt of this almost human talent to amuse. After setting up the tripod and camera so that a very expensive lens protruded slightly into the paddock, watched intently by *The Minstrel* all the while, the photographer entered the paddock and was lured by *The Minstrel* to the farthest corner. Once there the chestnut raced at high speed to the opposite side. The photographer feared the worst, expecting him to kick, bite or otherwise smash the thousands of dollars worth of glass. But *The Minstrel* only licked the lens profusely, raced back to the photographer, now in a state of near-shock, and presented himself, all innocence, for the photographic session.

The enthusiasm that *The Minstrel* showed on the

racecourse and now shows in the paddock is also very evident in the breeding shed. His yearlings will soon be in the sales, joining those of *Nijinsky II* and *Northern Dancer*. Though nothing is ever certain in the world of the thoroughbred, it is more than possible that *The Minstrel*'s offspring will share the brilliant qualities shown by the offspring of his half-brother and sire. Many are waiting with great anticipation for his two-year-olds to race in 1981. Many already suspect that they will prove to be champions.

Nijinsky II
Northern Dancer
Red Rum
Seattle Slew

Little *Northern Dancer* is one of the finest horses ever raised in Canada and one of the finest sires standing at stud in the world today. A Kentucky Derby winner in 1964, he sired *Nijinsky II*, the first horse to win the British Triple Crown in 35 years.

Red Rum was the hero of the Grand National Steeplechase at Aintree three times, a record making *Rum* as resolute as any horse in history. *Seattle Slew* became the tenth winner of American racing's Triple Crown. A horse so unheralded at the beginning and so accomplished at the end, he was possessed with blinding speed on the track, yet had the temperament of a child's pet.

Nijinsky II stands at stud
at Claiborne

When trainer Vincent O'Brien came to Windfields
to inspect a *Ribot* yearling for Charlie Engelhard,
he did not like what he saw. What he did like
was a *Northern Dancer* colt, a big rangy type that
could perhaps develop with time. The colt did.

His name was Nijinsky II.

Northern Dancer

Canada's *Northern Dancer* was a small horse with great natural speed. His Kentucky Derby victory was the fastest until *Secretariat*. He ran as if possessed, bounding along with tremendous energy and courage.

In twelve seasons at stud to the end of the seventies, twenty percent of the horses he sired became stakes winners, 68 in all, including *Nijinsky II* and *The Minstrel*, two English Derby winners. His son *Lyphard* sired *Three Troika's*, heroine of the 1979 Arc and conqueror of two champions, *Troy* and *Le Marmot*.

He stands at E.P. Taylor's Windfields Farm in Maryland. Each of the 32 syndication shares represents one service a breeding season and is now valued in excess of $200,000. This is with no guarantee of a live foal.

His influence in the world of racing is staggering.

It is one of thoroughbred racing's great ironies that at E.P. Taylor's annual private sale the tiny yearling later named *Northern Dancer* could not even command the reserve bid price of $25,000. To the knowledgeable buyers of potential champions, he was too small for consideration.

What he may have lacked in physical stature he more than compensated for on the track and in the breeding shed.

A great racehorse of the sixties, *Northern Dancer* became a sire of undisputed excellence in the seventies.

King of the Grand National

Red Rum's retirement at Ginger McCain's yard in Southport near Liverpool is anything but quiet. Most mornings *Rum* goes for a gallop on the local beach just as he did when he was in training. And now, as then, he looks magnificent.

He is in every way a celebrity and when not at home he is busy opening supermarkets or attending sporting events. He was even a mystery guest on the British television program "The Generation Game". In a very human way, he revels in the affection and attention he is shown.

The McCain children, Donald and Joanna, keep *Rum* well supplied with hugs and Polo mints and also see that his musical needs are met. When they play his favourite record, "Red Rum's Song", with the volume at full blast, he pokes his head out of his stall, ears cocked, then listens with rapt attention until the last strains die away over the cobblestones.

Red Rum is a familiar sight on the narrow streets of Southport as he heads down to the beach for his early morning gallop in the company of several of his stable companions. People stop to wave or just to admire his still fit form. Where the beach and sea merge the clock is turned back, and it is *Red Rum* racing the waves, preparing for yet another epic effort in Aintree's Grand National.

Seattle Slew

He was big and gangling and awkward, so they nick-named him 'Baby Huey' after the cartoon duck. Now that he is home from the races he's filled out. The gentleness is still there, as is the greatness. He looks every inch a Triple Crown winner.

On the racetrack his
action was faultless,
his acceleration awesome.

His races were full of
determination. If ever
a horse loved to run,
it was *Seattle Slew*.

Nijinsky II

For a few brief months in the summer of 1970, a horse from Canada was compared with *Ribot* of Italy and *Sea-Bird* of France. *Nijinsky II*, for a small span of time, was called the Horse of the Century.

Nijinsky II came from the successful breeding of two Queen's Plate winners, *Northern Dancer* and *Flaming Page*. He was bred by E.P. Taylor and was foaled in 1967 on Taylor's Windfields Farm in Oshawa, Canada. One year later, Taylor consigned him to the Canadian Thoroughbred Horse Society's annual yearling sale where he first made news; Fasig-Tipton's auctioneers sold him for the record price of $84,000. The buyer was Charles Engelhard, an American who in less than a decade had become one of racing's most celebrated owners on an international scale.

Engelhard wanted nothing more than to see his green, yellow and scarlet colours carried to victory in the Derby Stakes at Epsom. With this objective in mind, he had *Nijinsky II* shipped to Vincent O'Brien at Ballydoyle, near Cashel in County Tipperary. In was there on Irish ground that *Nijinsky II* learned how to run.

He was a big, strong colt. A bay, he looked more like his dam than his already illustrious sire. His disposition was very good, though for the first ten days in Ireland he steadfastly refused to eat the oats and hay given him. O'Brien, suspecting he had been raised on nuts, had his suspicions confirmed and promptly ordered nuts. But hunger solved the problem before they arrived; *Nijinsky II* learned to eat oats.

He put in a good winter, and it soon became evident that he could be a top performer. He showed that he could be handled without difficulty, and he showed an ability to vary his speed. The style with which he went from one gear to the next was flawless, and he displayed an exciting acceleration that only his riders could fully appreciate.

He was ready for the races on July 12, 1969 in the Erne Stakes, a six-furlong race for two-year-olds at the Curragh. Liam Ward, Ireland's champion jockey, had the mount and had no trouble riding *Nijinsky II* to an easy half a length victory over four rivals. One month later, he returned to the Curragh for the six-furlong, 63-yard Railway Stakes, and showed a fine turn of speed. The going was a little soft, but *Nijinsky II* didn't mind. In a few short strides, he passed *Decies* and won easily by five lengths, again showing that ability to move at the precise time his rider wanted him to. The pace, whether fast or slow, made no difference to him.

Two weeks later, over the same distance in the Curragh's Anglesey Stakes, Ward used the same tactics, keeping his horse in behind the leaders until the final furlong when he was quickly brought out into the clear. Then, with very little effort, he rushed by the leaders, winning by three lengths over *Everyday* and *Walky Talky*. He completed his Curragh engagements in September with a start in the one-mile Beresford Stakes. *Decies* ran a good race, but *Nijinsky II* used the final furlong to beat him by three-quarters of a length. The ground was soft and Ward had to shake him up, not with his whip, but more with hands and boots, just to keep him going.

Four wins in four races, and one at a mile, would satisfy most trainers with a good prospect, but O'Brien couldn't resist the temptation of a trip to England for *Nijinsky II* 's final start in 1969. At Newmarket, in the seven-furlong Dewhurst Stakes, Lester Piggott was up and *Nijinsky II* was never off a tight rein. Piggott never really let him run, but he still beat *Recalled* and *Sandal* so convincingly that he earned the honour of being champion two-year-old of both England and Ireland.

Five wins in five races, with only one posing any problems for the rider, was an excellent record, and, as he continued to thrive over the winter, there was much speculation about his potential in the Classics. Only one doubt remained. Did he have the necessary stamina? Many thought that his breeding would keep him from winning the Derby. True, *Nijinsky II* had great speed, maybe not a characteristic of a Classic stayer, but he also had the ability to relax and then pick up his pace in a most authoritative manner when asked.

Through the winter of 1969-1970, British pundits continually brought up his *Northern Dancer* bloodlines, remembering that *Northern Dancer* had failed in the Belmont Stakes at a mile and a half. But nobody writing or talking about the defeat ever mentioned that during the race *Northern Dancer* was held back so strongly that he could not overcome the prolonged heavy handling when Bill Hartack finally decided to let him run. *Nijinsky II* 's doubters either did not know about the Hartack ride or, if they did, chose to ignore it.

Even so, the pundits should have given more credit to Vincent O'Brien. If anyone could train this horse with the suspicious North American pedigree, it would be 'The Wizard of Cashel' who had already won two Derbies at Epsom. And *Nijinsky II* was a trainer's delight who enjoyed his work and never needed heavy training. It was a common sight to see him prick his ears once in front, and then just gallop away almost playfully. He excited those watching him by the way he did everything. O'Brien and *Nijinsky II* were a powerful combination

Nijinsky II made his first start as a three-year-old in the seven-furlong Gladness Stakes at the Curragh, where he won smartly from *Deep Run* and *Prince Tenderfoot*. It was a promising start to a season in which O'Brien's objectives were the great Classics of England.

First out was the first jewel in England's Triple Crown, the Two Thousand Guineas at Newmarket in April. Lester Piggott was back on *Nijinsky II*, and some of England's fastest horses were entered in the race. They went along at a very quick pace, but not quick enough. *Nijinsky II* showed tremendous speed and moved a little sooner than Piggott would have liked, but Piggott rode to O'Brien's orders, which were to avoid a late run with spectacular overtones. For most it was a good performance, but not for everybody. The doubts still lingered about the Derby, even though O'Brien declared that *Nijinsky II* was a better

horse than *Sir Ivor*. The bookmakers, at least, believed O'Brien, who had trained *Sir Ivor*, essentially a fine speed type, to get Epsom's mile and a half; they made *Nijinsky II* a certainty for the Derby.

On the day of the 191st Derby Stakes, the anticipation and excitement among the nearly half a million people in attendance were almost unbearable. As the field travelled along in a tight group, there in the middle was *Nijinsky II* with Piggott higher up than any ahead or behind. His position was just right, his view of the race was unobstructed and he was in complete command of his horse. When the field came around Tattenham Corner for the run through the straight, *Nijinsky II* was still well in behind, but closer. Through the dip in the straight, Piggott asked him to close up more. Suddenly *Gyr*, a giant French horse, went to the front two furlongs from home, and in another furlong *Stintino* made a great run along the outside. Still Piggott waited. With 150 yards to go, all of it uphill, he finally asked *Nijinsky II* to run. With a huge burst of speed, he went to the front and pulled away from the other strong closers, *Gyr* and *Stintino*, to finish with a time just off the course record. It was a brilliant performance, now considered one of the six most memorable in the Derby's two-century long history. The second jewel of the Crown was his.

He followed the victory with a good run in the Irish Sweeps Derby, again at a mile and half. It was the final ride for Liam Ward, who had an agreement with O'Brien to ride all his Irish starters, even if *Nijinsky II* with Piggott up won the Epsom Derby. Piggott was on *Meadowville*. *Nijinsky II* sweated quite freely, and for those who like their horses to be calm before a race, his appearance must have caused some concern that he would come unstuck the way so many English Derby winners had in the past. But such concern was unfounded. In the early running Ward kept *Nijinsky II* well back, just in behind Piggott on *Meadowville*. The two horses moved as one until they emerged with the leaders. Then, when *Nijinsky II* hit the front, Ward urged him on. The response was immediate. He shot ahead by three lengths and lived up to his notices beautifully.

In a month's time, he went back to England and Ascot for the King George VI and Queen Elizabeth Stakes. For the first time he faced older horses: *Blakeney*, the 1969 Epsom Derby winner; *Crepellano*, winner of the French Oaks; *Karabas*, the victor in the Washington, D.C., International; *Hogarth*, the Italian Derby winner; and *Caliban*, winner of the Coronation Cup. Some maintain that a horse is only as good as what he beats, and this is often used as a definition of the word "class". If so, *Nijinsky II* showed a great deal of class. It was another Classic at a mile and a half, and *Nijinsky II* just galloped along until Piggott asked him to turn on his speed. When he did, he simply roared past the impressive field. Piggott began to ease him, and *Blakeney* came up very fast towards the finish. But it was to no avail. *Nijinsky II* was easily in command.

After the King George VI, a highly contagious skin disease, ringworm, interrupted his Ballydoyle training, but despite this setback it was decided to try for the St. Leger, the final jewel in the Triple Crown. Once again, *Nijinsky II* returned to England with Piggott. The field he met at Doncaster was certainly not formidable, and the best account of the race was the one that simply said, "*Nijinsky II* cruised home on the bit." While winning against such a field was no great feat, the taking of the Triple Crown was stunning. No horse had claimed it since *Bahram* in 1935.

Now at the height of his success, with eleven wins in eleven starts, including five world Classics in a row, *Nijinsky II* was being compared with *Ribot* and *Sea-Bird*. He had been syndicated for a then world-record price of $5,440,000, and it was announced that his new home would be Claiborne Farm in Paris, Kentucky. But there were still races to be won.

Before crossing the Atlantic, *Nijinsky II* crossed the Channel to run in the world's richest race for thoroughbreds, the Prix de l'Arc de Triomphe at Longchamp. All that was needed for him to win was firm ground and no bad luck, but on the first Sunday in October the rains came. And so did Europe's best horses.

The belief that *Nijinsky II* was the horse of the century faded in the final furlong of the Arc. For suddenly *Nijinsky II* was at the front with Piggott, but so was *Sassafras* with Yves Saint-Martin, France's leading jockey and noted Arc expert. Piggott resorted to his whip, *Nijinsky II* swerved, *Sassafras* held firm and continued on. *Nijinsky II* could not stay with him, and at the wire it was *Sassafras* the winner by a head, with *Nijinsky II* and a shattered Piggott second.

Various reasons were suggested to explain why he lost. The army of photographers present while *Nijinsky II* was in the walking-ring made him extremely nervous; he seemed agitated and not right with himself. He was also the outside horse in a field of fifteen. Did he move too late

from too far back? Before the Arc Piggott had told O'Brien, "I don't care if there are a hundred horses in front of me." Did they have too much to do? Did Piggott bring him to the front too soon? It is clear that Piggott's choices were severely limited starting from the extreme outside of the field. A jockey can either use his horse early or stay at the rear and cross over late in the race, but either way there are serious problems for both horse and rider. *Nijinsky II* just could not overcome the outside position to beat *Sassafras* who saved ground from a good position and had no trouble with traffic.

There is nothing more lonely than a champion when he goes down to defeat for the first time. *Nijinsky II* for a short while had appeared to be in excellent shape, but after the Arc it was easy to conclude that the St. Leger had taken its toll. Piggott was not on the *Nijinsky II* of June and July when he rode to defeat in the Arc.

Sadly, *Nijinsky II* started one more time, in the mile and a quarter Champion Stakes at Newmarket. Again he was upset by the pre-race excitement and trembled noticeably going into the gate. *Lorenzaccio*, a good horse but not one of the top drawer, beat him easily. Subsequently, his managers felt they had failed him. After Ascot, when he lost training time because of ringworm he should have been withdrawn from either the St. Leger or the Arc. It's always the same in racing, however. Even those closest to the horse in question cannot always tell just when he's past his peak. Sometimes the horse fools people, because he continues to look and act like his old self. Such was the case with *Nijinsky II* .

Nevertheless, for a few months during one of Britain's finest summers, a Canadian horse owned by an American, trained by an Irishman and ridden by the best of England and Ireland, thrilled the people of the racing world. He was champion three-year-old of England and Ireland, Horse of the Year in Europe, and for some, for a few brief months, he was the Horse of the Century. For a very few, he was the handsome bay that came in by air to Shannon, then travelled by road to Ballydoyle to the cheers of the villagers of Cashel.

Now one of racing's most successful sires, *Nijinsky II*'s colts and fillies sell for record prices. In his paddock at Claiborne Farm in Kentucky, he plays, stops, starts, lifts his head, and leaves no doubt that he is still a champion.

Northern Dancer

Hyperion, the great English Derby winner of 1933, has had a profound influence on breeding throughout the world, with his name appearing in the bloodlines of champions on both sides of the Atlantic. Fortunately for Canadian racing, E. P. Taylor agreed to buy a *Hyperion* mare named *Lady Angela* in England. When he bought her she was in foal to the great *Nearco.* The result was *Empire Day,* not a promising looking individual at all. Taylor decided to try once more. With some difficulty, another service was secured to *Nearco,* and when *Lady Angela* was in foal again she was shipped to Canada, arriving by boat in Montreal with little *Empire Day* at her side. Her second foal from the mating with *Nearco* proved to be a great one. His name was *Nearctic,* a horse considered too speed crazy in racing, but one who became the most important sire to ever stand at stud in Canada.

Natalma was a daughter of *Native Dancer,* Alfred G. Vanderbilt's great grey of the early fifties, who won twenty-one of his twenty-two starts. When *Natalma* was forced out of racing because of injury, Taylor decided to breed her to *Nearctic,* even though it was late May. The result was a very tiny bay colt with a crooked stripe down his face and with three white feet. He was named *Northern Dancer.*

While he was a racehorse of the sixties, *Northern Dancer* has a place in the story of champions in the seventies because of his position as a sire of undisputed excellence. During the decade, his progeny carried his name to glory, glory that he, himself, once knew.

As a yearling in 1961 *Northern Dancer* was placed in Taylor's pre-priced yearling sale. Taylor's policy in those days was always to sell half of his colts and fillies and retain the rest. But *Northern Dancer*'s price of $25,000 discouraged some from buying, while others were put off by his small size. He was a leftover, a tiny reject that Taylor raced himself.

In August, 1963, *Northern Dancer* appeared at Fort Erie, Ontario in an eight-horse maiden two-year-old race at a distance of five and a half furlongs. It was his first start and he was the even-money favourite. In the saddle was an apprentice jockey named Ronnie Turcotte who rode him to an easy victory by six and three-quarter lengths. Both Turcotte and trainer Horatio Luro were impressed. Fifteen days later at Fort Erie he went down to his first defeat, beaten by *Ramblin Road,* a speedy American-bred, by four lengths over a distance of six and a half furlongs. But, with the benefit of two sprints, *Northern Dancer* came right back at the end of the month in the very demanding Summer Stakes, one mile on the turf. He took to the soft ground wonderfully, showing excellent speed throughout and winning by a length and a quarter.

He then travelled ninety miles back to Toronto for the big stakes for juveniles at the Woodbine Autumn meet, the Cup and Saucer Stakes, also on the turf, and the Coronation Futurity on the dirt. The races, the richest in Canada for two-year-olds, were worth over $35,000 each in first prize money. Under the conditions for the mile and a sixteenth Cup and Saucer Stakes, *Northern Dancer* carried 124 pounds and, try as Ronnie Turcotte might, he simply could not get home in front. He finished second, three-quarters of a length behind *Grand Garcon,* an enormous horse that Taylor had sold the year before, in one of Canadian racing's biggest upsets. *Grand Garcon* rewarded his backers with a 45–1 payoff, and gave the Taylor racing group plenty to wonder about.

Fifteen runners went for the prize in the Coronation Futurity at one mile and an eighth, but none could match

Northern Dancer's extraordinary strides. Breaking from the number ten stall, Turcotte got him nicely into position close to the early leaders, always under good restraint. He was already showing the signs of being a natural speed horse who could be rated. Going down the backstretch Turcotte moved *Northern Dancer* from fourth to the front just as the field was approaching the far turn. With five furlongs already covered, they moved away at will, travelling the final half-mile with speed to spare and winning ultimately by six and a half lengths. It was now clear that *Northern Dancer* would be the horse to beat in the Queen's Plate the following year.

Coronation Futurity winners usually went into winter quarters, but *Northern Dancer* was not through yet. On a cold, wet November day he started in Greenwood's Carlton Stakes. The track was muddy for the seven-furlong race, and Jim Fitzsimmons hustled him along the short-lane, tight-turn, three-quarter mile Greenwood track. *Northern Dancer* responded gamely, ran head-to-head most of the way and won by two and a half lengths over *Northern Flight* and *Winkie*.

Shipped to Aqueduct for a race on November 18th, he met a small field of six runners. The 6–5 favourite was a hard-running dark bay son of *Double Jay* named *Bupers* who had already earned his keep by winning the Futurity Stakes first prize of $90,974. In the early running Manuel Ycaza kept *Northern Dancer* back in fourth position, about five lengths behind the leaders. When Ycaza turned him loose he made one explosive breathtaking run that produced an eight-length victory over a tired *Bupers*. The race was carded as a tune-up for the one-mile Remsen Stakes on November 27th in which *Northern Dancer* carried top weight of 124 pounds, giving away chunks of weight to the other five runners. This time Ycaza let him run early. *Northern Dancer* made nearly all the pace under light restraint and won by two lengths.

Northern Dancer had now won on the front end giving away weight to all his rivals, and he had come from behind at equal weights. He had started nine times, won seven, and had been second in two, for total earnings of $90,635. He had won in Canada from five and a half furlongs to a mile and an eighth, on both dirt and turf, and had won in New York twice at a mile, both races in good time. What stood out was that he had won six races over a distance of ground. The little late foal was still tiny at two, but everyone agreed he could run.

For a short time in the early winter he went through a crisis with a quarter crack, a crack in the wall of the hoof. A blacksmith named Bane from California had a remedy for such a situation that had already worked successfully on a good harness horse, so Bane was brought east. In simple terms, he vulcanized the hoof with a special patch. *Northern Dancer* responded to the treatment perfectly, and with good care and some rest he was soon ready for his three-year-old season.

Canada's champion two-year-old colt started to bloom and fill out under the warm Florida sun. He had endless visitors to his barn at Hialeah, and none were so hopeful as the Taylor entourage. *Northern Dancer* had shown a tremendous will to run. Now, if only he could continue to mature and develop there was a strong chance he could be a serious threat in the three-year-old Classics of American racing. To this end his talented and wily trainer, Horatio Luro, put all of his knowledge and experience. Luro had trained *Decidedly*, the 1962 Kentucky Derby winner, and knew the road to Louisville first hand.

The two main winter objectives were the Flamingo Stakes at Hialeah and the Florida Derby at Gulfstream, both at a mile and an eighth and both calling for equal weights of 122 pounds. *Northern Dancer* trained well and made his first start of the season in a six-furlong sprint at Hialeah on February 10th. The best he could manage was a third, two lengths behind the winner, *Chieftain*. The defeat was a blow to the pride of those who visualize champions always winning, but the race was just part of the training program that resulted in ultimate success on March 3rd in the $100,000 Flamingo Stakes, Hialeah's star attraction.

Flamingo winners were often America's champions. *Never Bend*, *Mill Reef*'s sire, had won the Flamingo in 1963, and in earlier years so had *Bold Ruler*, *Secretariat*'s sire, *Nashua*, and *Citation*. In 1964 the track was fast, and so was the race. *Mr. Brick* led the eleven-horse field with a half in :45-3/5 and a three-quarters in 1:09-2/5. *Northern Dancer* with the great Bill Shoemaker stayed right behind him, forcing him all the way. Shoemaker had a difficult ride, because as he advanced on the outside *Northern Dancer* continually lugged-in. Shoemaker's left-handed whipping straightened him, keeping him off *Mr. Brick* until they passed him, but the lugging-in continued as they raced to the wire in a driving finish that saw *Northern Dancer* beat *Mr. Brick* by two lengths in 1:47-4/5, only 4/5 off *Bold Ruler*'s track record. Despite the lugging-in performance, many people began to see *Northern Dancer* as a possible winner on the first Saturday in May. One person who did not was jockey Bill Shoemaker, but it took some time before he said so.

Over at Gulfstream Park, Luro went back to sprinting *Northern Dancer*. He blazed seven furlongs on March 28th in 1:22-2/5, equalling the track record, and was now tuned to a concert pitch for the $100,000 Florida Derby, Gulfstream's three-year-old Classic. Eight horses went to the post, and the public made *Northern Dancer* a heavy favourite at 3–10. Shoemaker this time had an easy ride. They got away in good order, followed the very slow pace of *Greek Episode* with no trouble, then turning into the stretch took the lead in a few quick strides. *Northern Dancer* won by a length over *The Scoundrel* in the very slow time of 1:50-4/5, four full seconds off the track record.

Shoemaker now announced that in the Kentucky Derby he would ride the California champion *Hill Rise* who had won the Santa Anita Derby by six lengths. Horatio Luro's response was to engage Bill Hartack, who had won the Derby two years before for Luro on *Decidedly* and had also won on *Venetian Way* in 1960 and *Iron Liege* in 1957. The new combination of horse and rider was tried out in the Blue Grass Stakes at Keeneland, Kentucky nine days before the Derby. Only five runners were entered, and *Northern Dancer* was hard-held off a very slow pace throughout the early running. He moved on the outside on the final turn, then when challenged in the stretch he moved again. The Daily Racing Form chart caller noted that *Northern Dancer* "won the Blue Grass cleverly". Hartack had saved his mount's resources, and had already taught him to move when he wanted. The new combination looked good.

At Churchill Downs there was something unusual about the huge crowd that cheered after the band had finished playing 'My Old Kentucky Home'. Thousands were Canadians, and most of them had to wonder if what they were hoping for could really come true. When the twelve horses for the 90th Derby reached the gate, Canada waited with hope and expectation. And so did E. P. Taylor, who had said for decades that he would one day have a horse that could win the Kentucky Derby. Only months before, his good friend, A. B. 'Bull' Hancock, father of the present master of Claiborne Farm, had half-seriously told Taylor that if he wanted to win any money he should stay in Canada and forget Kentucky. Taylor had chuckled at the good-natured ribbing, but now he wanted to have the last laugh.

Hill Rise was the favourite at 7–5, and *Northern Dancer* was a strong second choice at 7–2. The start was good with *Royal Shuck* and *Mr. Brick* getting away fast. *Wil Rad* and *The Scoundrel* were also early leaders. *Northern Dancer*, who had broken from the number seven stall, was over on the rail in a contending position. *Hill Rise* had been

bumped by *The Scoundrel*, but was now settling down for Shoemaker in the run into the first turn. Hartack kept *Northern Dancer* on the inside under a very strong hold, saving all possible ground. After six furlongs he let him run. When there was no more room, he had to come out midway off the far turn. Turning into the stretch with a quarter of a mile to go Hartack and *Northern Dancer* were in front; the quick acceleration of the tiny colt had rocketed him into a clear lead. But the inevitable finally happened. Shoemaker and *Hill Rise*, after a steady run from the half-mile pole, were suddenly on the extreme outside and closing. Hartack went to tough left-handed whipping and little *Northern Dancer* came on, his every stride strongly keeping him in front as *Hill Rise* closed the gap. Shoemaker did everything he possibly could, but *Hill Rise* simply could not get there. *Northern Dancer* held him even and won by a long neck in new track record time of 2:00 flat for the mile and a quarter.

Back in Canada an entire population identified with the pride of the Taylors as they went to the winner's circle. *Northern Dancer*, the first Canadian-bred to ever win the Derby, was now Canada's horse. The emotionalism of the moment totally upstaged the hard realities of the pari-mutuels, but for those who had invested *Northern Dancer* paid $8.80 for $2.00. Thousands of bettors felt lucky and rich, the rarest of combinations, and the finest.

Northern Dancer had now beaten the best in American racing, but there were still some who doubted his ability. Their numbers diminished considerably two weeks later as *Northern Dancer* in a powerful display won the Preakness Stakes at Pimlico. This time he won in the clear by two and a quarter lengths, with *The Scoundrel* in second, a head in front of *Hill Rise*. One more race and the Triple Crown could be taken out of America for the very first time.

The 96th running of the Belmont Stakes took place at Aqueduct; Belmont was closed for renovations. Seven other horses were in the gate placed on the far turn. *Northern Dancer* had drawn the number two stall. Luro instructed Hartack to wait, and that's what Hartack did. *Orientalist* set a slow pace for the first mile, until *Quadrangle*, who had been fifth in the Derby and fourth in the Preakness, took over. Down the backstretch Hartack took another hold on *Northern Dancer*, a hold so strong that he was running with his mouth wide open. Finally, Hartack went from a pull to a drive. Turning into the stretch *Northern Dancer* was right there with *Quadrangle,* but then it was all over. Manuel Ycaza briskly urged *Quadrangle* to pull away and the race was his by two lengths. *Roman Brother* was second, four lengths ahead of a tired *Northern Dancer.*

The Belmont had been a very bad experience. *Northern Dancer* coughed up sand and dirt for nearly two hours afterwards. It was now clear that *Quadrangle* could be rated. His trainer had even said so publicly when asked at the pre-race breakfast, but Luro had not heard this comment. If he had, his instructions to Hartack might have been different and the Triple Crown might have been his. *Northern Dancer* raced under 'double wraps' because of the very slow early pace, and could not do his best.

He went back home to Toronto for his last hurrah at Woodbine in the 105th Queen's Plate at a mile and a quarter. Only seven runners opposed him. When the field entered the walking-ring on the way to the paddock, *Northern Dancer* stopped, stood still, then reared up on his hind legs as if to acknowledge the cheers of the crowd. In the race he didn't disappoint them. After a rather desperate beginning where he was momentarily blocked, he squeezed through the narrowest of openings and won easily by seven and a half lengths.

It was the last time he raced in the Windfields turquoise and gold, for a few weeks later while training for the Travers at Belmont he wrapped a tendon on his left foreleg which eventually bowed. He was never in serious training again, though he did make one more run down the Woodbine track. After the fourth race on October 24th, the day of the Canadian Championship, *Northern Dancer* came out alone and galloped past the stands to say goodbye.

In 1964 *Northern Dancer* raced nine times, won seven, and was third in two for earnings of $490,171. He won five American Classic races in a row and was named Canada's Horse of the Year and America's three-year-old champion. One career was over, and another was to begin. He was retired to stud at Taylor's farm in Oshawa where he remained until 1970 when he was syndicated for $2,400,000 and transferred to the Windfields Farm in Chesapeake City, Maryland.

In the thoroughbred horse breeding business stallions who sire ten per cent stakes winners are considered successful. In twelve seasons *Northern Dancer* has sired twenty per cent, 68 stakes winners in 338 foals.

From the beginning the *Northern Dancer*s have been exceptional. *Viceregal* was Canada's Horse of the Year in

1968, the game mare *Fanfreluche,* who later gained some notoriety by being kidnapped while in foal to *Secretariat,* was Horse of the Year in 1970 and *Laurie's Dancer* received the same honour in 1971.

Nijinsky II was the best advertisement *Northern Dancer* and Canadian breeding could ever have. His eleven-race sweep included five world Classics, the Two Thousand Guineas Stakes, the Derby Stakes, The Irish Sweeps Derby, the King George VI and Queen Elizabeth Stakes, and the St. Leger Stakes. He was the first horse to win England's Triple Crown in thirty-five years and until he lost the Prix de l'Arc de Triomphe by a head many thought he was the Horse of the Century. He was Europe's Horse of the Year in 1970, and at the end of the seventies his earnings of $677,177 still make him the leading Canadian-bred money winner of all time. Retired to Claiborne Farm in Kentucky, he is now a star at stud. His good son *Ile de Bourbon* won the King George VI and Queen Elizabeth Diamond Stakes at Ascot in 1978 as he himself did in 1970. In 1980 much is expected of his colt *Nice Havrais* and his filly *Princess Lida,* as well as *Aryenne* by his son *Green Dancer.* *Nijinsky II* was two-year-old sire in Europe in 1979.

Another *Northern Dancer* to win the Epsom Derby was *The Minstrel.* He was undefeated at two and won four of his six starts at three. His defeat of *Blushing Groom* in the Derby was decisive, but his greatest race came when he outgamed *Orange Bay* in the King George VI and Queen Elizabeth Diamond Stakes. Like *Nijinsky II* and *Ile de Bourbon,* he was a three-year-old racing against older horses when he accomplished this feat. *The Minstrel* was named European Horse of the Year in 1977, and commenced stud duties at Windfields Farm in Maryland in 1978.

Lyphard, a 1969 foal by *Northern Dancer* from the *Court Martial* mare *Goofed,* was not the very best on the racecourse, but at stud he's become one of the world's hottest sires. His great filly *Three Troikas* won the last Arc of the seventies, easily beating *Le Marmot,* France's champion three-year-old, and England's champion *Troy.*

In the 1978 Keeneland Sales in Lexington, Kentucky, a *Northern Dancer* colt later named *Nureyev* was sold by Claiborne Farm for $1,300,000 to Stavros Niarchos. *Nureyev* was one of French racing's most promising juveniles in 1979 and much is expected of him in 1980. Much is also expected of the fine ten-furlong specialist

Northern Baby who won stakes in both France and England in 1979.

Northern Dancer's daughters have also shone. Besides *Fanfreluche*, there was *Alma North*, a bay from the *Swaps* mare *Spaws Arrow*, who made a mark in the early seventies by winning stakes at Delaware, Monmouth, Liberty Bell, Atlantic City, Garden State, Pimlico and Bowie.

One of his bargain fillies was *Northernette*. A $50,000 yearling, she was Canada's champion two-year-old filly in 1976 and three-year-old champion filly in 1977. At three, she won the rich Canadian Oak Stakes by eleven lengths in the slop, then came back one week later to finish a game second to *Sound Reason* in the Queen's Plate, Canada's blue-ribbon race for three-year-olds. Sold to Peter Brant and raced in the United States, she finished second in the Test Stakes at Saratoga and first in the nine-furlong Chrysanthemum Handicap at Laurel. She earned $173,193 as a three-year-old and did even better at four. In 1978 she won Oaklawn Park's rich Apple Blossom and Aqueduct's famous Top Flight. Her year's earnings totalled $180,867. As a broodmare *Northernette* is now worth well over $1,000,000.

The list could go on much further and will continue to expand in the eighties, because at twenty years of age *Northern Dancer* is still at work passing on his speed and greatness. There are many who would claim *Northern Dancer* to be the greatest sire of the seventies. Some even believe his influence may someday rival that of his great-grand-sire *Hyperion*. Whatever the final judgement, *Northern Dancer* will long be remembered in the racing world for the excellence of his offspring.

But there are millions of people in Canada, completely unaware of his record as a sire, who still remember proudly how with courage and speed their little bay colt won a race as great as the Kentucky Derby. The hopes of a country rode with him on that wonderful day in May, and the spirits of a country were lifted high when he crossed the wire in front. If he had never run another race and never sired a horse, Canadians even to this day would say his name with love.

Red Rum

While horseracing is enjoyed in most countries of the world, nowhere are fine horses recognized and loved so much as they are in Britain. One attribute that distinguishes British racing enthusiasts from, say, their American counterparts, is that their appreciation is not limited to runners on the flat. Most Americans may thrill to the annual Triple Crown saga, but would draw a blank if asked to name a champion jumper. The British, however, recognize in jumpers not only strength, endurance, training and ability, but tremendous courage as well.

To show such qualities, Britain has many tests, but none is greater than the Grand National Steeplechase for horses six years old and upward. The Grand National is a popular British institution that cannot be compared to any other event in the world. Eighteen BBC cameras, including one on a specially built moving vehicle that travels down a straight road beside the course, capture the feeling of the event for the millions who annually tune in.

First run over the historic Aintree course at Liverpool in 1839, the Grand National has thirty jumps, sixteen on the first circuit, fourteen on the second. The famous Chair Jump and the Water Jump are negotiated only on the first circuit. The Liverpool fences are unusual. Thorn-dressed with fir, they are designed to stop a horse if he hits them. Many of the jumps are taller than regulation fences, and eight of them stand five feet high, with landing sides lower than the take-off sides. One of these, the third jump, has a six-foot open ditch. Becher's Brook is five feet, six inches wide, with a fence four feet, ten inches high, and the Canal Turn has a five-foot jump on a very tight left-handed bend. For good measure, there's the Chair, a six-foot ditch with a fence at five feet, two inches.

The jump after Becher's Brook is only a four-foot one, but it is on an angle with no drop on the landing side. This jump always surprises, while the others simply terrify. "In the Grand National the jumps just get taller and taller as you approach them. On the second circuit some of them seem even taller than on the first." It is no wonder that the jockeys who ride in the Grand National are called the 'suicide boys' by their fellow flat riders.

In the near-century and a half that it has been run only six horses have won the Grand National twice. Only one horse has ever won it three times. The three-time winner was *Red Rum,* whose amazing finish over the great Australian *Crisp* in 1973 is one of the most memorable Grand Nationals of all time. He is justly famous throughout Britain, and his fame was earned the hard way. His story is very much like an original screenplay, made up of the wistful, the comic and the utterly fantastic.

The screenplay would open with a shot of a young lad from Liverpool making his first bet on a Grand National in 1906. The lad would be Noel Le Mare, who that day had a dream of owning a horse good enough to win the great race. It would close with a scene sixty-seven years later when the dream was finally realized. In between would be the story of an unpromising horse who struggled to become great.

For a stud fee of only £198, Martin McEnerny of Kilkenny, Ireland bred his mare *Mared* to *Quorum* at Balreask Stud in the spring of 1964. The foal that arrived was a bay like his mother, was on the small side, and was named *Red Rum.* As a yearling he was put up for sale at the famous Ballsbridge Autumn Sales in Dublin and made a most inauspicious debut in the world of racing. As bad luck would have it, he fell over in his box and hurt himself. He wasn't too sore, but he was stiff, and for the very few prospective buyers on hand he was not an attractive proposition. McEnerny had a reserve bid on him of 800 guineas, but when he saw how little bidding there was he let him go for 400.

Maurice Kingsley of Manchester was *Red Rum*'s new owner, and he agreed to him being gelded because he seemed a handful, just too rambunctious a colt for serious training. In 1967 he made his first start on the flat over the Aintree course at Liverpool on April 7th. The race was the Thursby Selling Plate at five furlongs, and he won, but in a dead-heat with *Curlicue*. Even so, he earned £133.80 for his new owner and confirmed trainer Tim Molony's belief that he really could win. The dead-heat was a disappointment, however, and it was followed by trips to Beverley, then Teeside where he ran unplaced. At Newcastle he finished third in the six-furlong Angerton Stakes and earned £62.70, then picked up £467.00 at Warwick when he won the seven-furlong Pinley Nursery Handicap Stakes. He was unplaced at York, third at Pontefract in a one-mile race for a £60.00 purse, and finished the season at Leicester on September 24th with a fourth-place finish.

In 1968 *Red Rum* made only two starts on the flat. The first was on March 27th at Doncaster in the seven-furlong Waterdale Selling Handicap, and, with Geoff Lewis up, he won by a short head carrying the top weight. Three days later, on March 30th, he lost the Earl of Sefton's Stakes. His Doncaster win had resulted in a 10 pound penalty, and even the great Lester Piggott in the saddle couldn't help. That same day at Aintree *Red Alligator* and jockey Brian Fletcher won the Grand National Steeplechase.

Bobby Renton, a great 'chasing' trainer, bought *Red Rum* that spring, and that was the end of his days on the flat. He was sent to Oxclose where he became acquainted with Irish jockey Tommy Stack, head lad Charlie Wright, and, most important, Sandra Kendall who became his inseparable partner and loving teacher. It was time to go to school. When it came to his 'chasing' lessons *Red Rum* handled everything with ease. Sandra Kendall patiently taught him what he needed to know, and he showed talent. It didn't matter what the obstacles were, small hurdles or big hurdles, "He just flew over them really fast."

On September 18th, *'Rummy'* made his first start as a 'chaser' at Cheltenham in the Junior Novices' Hurdle at two miles and finished second, beaten by four lengths. His prize money was £90.00. Through the winter he started at Market Rasen, Nottingham, Doncaster, and Wetherby. By March 27th he was at Liverpool for the Lancashire Hurdle Race, two miles and 100 yards, where he finished

second. On April 7th, he won the Bilton Hurdle Handicap at two miles, then won two more races over the hurdles at Nottingham and Teeside, finishing out the 1968-69 season unplaced at Ayr.

It had been a moderately promising beginning, but *Red Rum* then went into a very bad slump. In the 1969-70 season he started fourteen times and failed to win, although he did manage two seconds and a third. In the 1970-71 season he raced thirteen times in steeplechases, not hurdles, and won only once, with no seconds, but seven thirds. He suffered greatly from a virus the year before, and the disease must have taken its toll. He just wasn't himself. In January, 1972 the veterinarians were called in and they diagnosed his condition as chronic pedalosteitis–*Red Rum* had very painful arthritis. Still, he managed two moderate wins in the 1971-72 steeplechase season, both of them at Catterick and both at three miles and 300 yards. Robert Benton had *Red Rum* going well now, so it was a surprise when he put him in the Doncaster Sales.

Noel Le Mare had often discussed his Aintree dream with trainer Donald 'Ginger' McCain and had asked McCain to be on the lookout for a potential Grand National winner. McCain was in the ring at Doncaster with instructions to go to 7,000 guineas for a prospect, if he had to. *Red Rum*'s presence stimulated enough bidding to get the price up to 5,500. McCain, an experienced former car dealer, knew that to top it with a jump to 6,000 might be just enough to make his bid the successful one. He was right. *Red Rum* was sold to Noel Le Mare, and shipped immediately to McCain's yard at Southport.

The Southport sands were soon used for 'Rummy''s gallops, but not before endless walks in the sea cured the lameness he had when he arrived. The sea was a tonic, for in the 1972-73 season *Red Rum* finally made his mark in the racing world. Through the fall he won in the North at Carlisle, then at Wetherby, Newcastle, and Haydock. With four steeplechase wins in four starts, all of them at three miles or longer, it suddenly seemed that with Ginger McCain's touch, *Red Rum* could realize Noel Le Mare's dream.

One of the many who took notice of *Red Rum*'s winning streak was Jockey Brian Fletcher, who had won the 1968 Grand National on *Red Alligator*. Fletcher had ridden a few horses for McCain and was presently in a very bad way. He had fractured his skull in a nasty fall at Teeside Park and many wondered if he had lost his nerve. He was most anxious to make a big comeback, but he needed a big horse. Jockeys are very much like performers; they're only as good as their last show. Fletcher needed another

Red Alligator at Aintree. As luck would have it, regular rider Tommy Stack could not ride *Red Rum* for a race at Ayr, the Mauchline Handicap Chase. Fletcher approached McCain and asked if he could have the mount. The answer was yes. On the afternoon of November 13th, *Red Rum* won his fifth race at Ayr, this time with Brian Fletcher.

Fletcher was now booked to ride *Red Rum* in the 1973 Grand National Steeplechase on March 31st. The morning of the race, 'Ginger' McCain worked *Red Rum*, in company with *Glenkiln*, over a distance of about six furlongs on the wet Southport sands. When they pulled up 'Rummy' was blowing, blowing so much that McCain had him do the work again. It's a bad sign when a horse is out of breath, and it seemed an incredible decision to work a horse twice at sprint distances the morning of the race. A thoroughbred trainer would have to be mad to try such a thing, and a steeplechase trainer preparing a 'chaser' for four miles and 865 yards would have to know exactly what he was doing. There could be absolutely no margin for an error in such a situation. This workout was wisely not mentioned to Fletcher before the race. McCain correctly figured that his jockey would have quite enough to do without worrying about the training.

Before the race, Noel Le Mare, ever nearer his dream being realized, told Brian Fletcher, "Win if you can, but come home safe." Fletcher was determined to do both. Thirty-eight horses went to the post, with *Red Rum* and a giant Australian horse, *Crisp*, co-favourites at 9–1. *Red Rum* was getting 23 pounds from *Crisp*, which meant that *Crisp* was in with a staggering 168 pounds. No horse since the wonderful *Reynoldstown* had carried such a steadying burden.

After the fourth fence, with twenty-six to go, *Crisp* started to run away from his field. The first circuit is never taken too seriously by experienced Aintree specialists. It's always hoped that a heavy toll will be taken before the second circuit, so the best idea is to avoid trouble and save the horse. Fletcher waited until the third fence on the second circuit, jump 19, then figured it was time to go after *Crisp*. At the famous Valentine's Brook, *Crisp* was almost out of sight. He was jumping superbly, but so was *Red Rum*. At Becher's Brook on the second circuit, *Crisp's* lead was now more than 100 yards clear. With one mile to go the task seemed hopeless, for nothing was changing.

Suddenly, just after jump 29, but before jump 30, *Crisp* lost his smooth flow and started to reel, but he still had an enormous lead. Fletcher said that it was only at this time that he really felt encouraged. Noel Le Mare's dream had but one horse in the way. At the last fence it

was *Crisp* driving now by ten lengths, with *Red Rum* making up ground rapidly. The enormous Aintree crowd stirred to the occasion, as did millions watching on television, for they knew that a terrible struggle between a giant Australian horse and what looked like a small Irish-bred behind him was now about to take place. *Crisp* was so tired that he nearly staggered into the rails. *Red Rum* still had far too much to do, but he was determined, running on as if there was never going to be another race. Fletcher urged him on, still desperately hoping that the winning post would not arrive too soon. Dick Pitman could do nothing on *Crisp* but hope that the finish would not be too late.

With 100 yards to go *Crisp* had the race; he was all-in, but he had built up too big a lead. With 75 yards to go *Red Rum* looked now to be just too late when it really counted. With 50 yards to the wire the thought flashed through Fletcher's mind that he actually might win. With a few strides to go *Red Rum* caught *Crisp* and with a final, unimaginable effort put him away and won.

Noel Le Mare, at the age of eighty-five, was almost speechless as he revelled in his moment. 'Ginger' McCain's daring training trials that morning had tightened 'Rummy' up for the race of his life. The win was also an elixir for Brian Fletcher and vaulted him to the top of the steeplechasing world, a world with its own uniquely exciting rewards.

The winning trio of Le Mare, McCain and Fletcher stayed together for an historic encore in 1974. It was *Red Rum's* turn to carry 168 pounds in the Grand National, and he won with incredible power. The great *L'Escargot* was second, seven lengths behind. Brian Fletcher stood up in the stirrups to acknowledge the cheers of the crowd. He was now the second jockey in the twentieth century to win three Grand Nationals. Only Ernie Piggott, Lester Piggott's grandfather, had done it before, in 1912, 1918, and 1919. And *Red Rum* made even more steeplechase racing history three weeks later by winning the four mile, 120-yard Scottish Grand National at Ayr, making a rare double.

The ground had been firm for the 1973 and 1974 Grand Nationals, but in 1975 the rains came. With the going less than ideal, the chance for a 'Rummy' triple was lost, but he and Fletcher did manage a gallant second to *L'Escargot* with Tommy Carberry. It was the last time that Brian Fletcher would ride *Red Rum* in the Grand National. As so often happens in racing, a rider change was made. For Brian Fletcher the parting of the ways was almost impossible to accept, for he truly loved *Red Rum*. Trainer 'Ginger' McCain loved *Red Rum* as well, and strongly felt his gallant old champion would do better with another jockey.

In the 1976 Grand National Tommy Stack rode the 'Old King of Aintree' to a second-place finish behind *Rag Trade*. It was another courageous and amazing performance, but it did not match the momentous drama that unfolded in the 1977 Grand National. Tommy Stack was on *'Rummy'* again. The old boy was twelve years old, but it didn't matter this final time. In a gruelling renewal, all of it over familiar Aintree ground, *Red Rum* won the world's most difficult steeplechase for the third time, rewarding his backers with a 9–1 payoff by beating *Churchtown Boy* and *Eyecatcher*.

It was the end of an incredible campaign. In 110 life-time starts, 100 of them over hurdle and steeplechase courses, he won twenty-seven races, placed second in fifteen and finished third in twenty-three for total earnings of £146,409.80.

He is still at Southport near Liverpool, where he still goes out for morning gallops on the sands. He is also still a television star whose last appearance was not from a racecourse, but from a television studio where he was a guest on a quiz program, 'The Generation Game'. Having thrilled Britons with his victories at an age when flat runners would have long since been retired, he still gets lots of mail from people for whom he will always be the great Steeplechase Champion, the horse that rode out of Noel Le Mare's dream and made that dream reality.

Seattle Slew

Early in 1977 a horse with a rather unusual name and owned by people relatively new to racing started to attract some serious attention. As a yearling he had cost only $17,500 at a public auction. At the races as a two-year-old he had started only three times, but had raced well enough to be judged champion two-year-old colt of America. His most loyal supporters, and there were many, could see him becoming the tenth American Triple Crown winner. Amazingly, the value of this still undefeated horse would skyrocket to $12,000,000 if he lived up to his notices. His name was *Seattle Slew*.

He was a dark bay or brown colt and he first saw the world early in the evening on February 15, 1974, on Ben S. Castleman's modest White Horse Acres Farm in Lexington, Kentucky. Like so many horses, both good and bad, *Seattle Slew* was more the result of luck than careful planning. Castleman, a retired restauranteur who had been around racing people for more than three decades, wanted to breed his five-year-old mare *My Charmer* to *Jacinto*, one of twenty-five stallions down the road at the world famous Claiborne Farm. Seth Hancock, the master of Claiborne, was unable to help. *Jacinto's* book was full and Castleman was too late. However, there was a brand new stud starting out named *Bold Reasoning*, and his fee was just right for Castleman, only $5,000. What turned out to be another historic mating at Claiborne took place in March, 1973.

Seattle Slew was a big, awkward-looking colt, gangling and uncoordinated, but with a wonderful disposition like his mother. As a yearling he was still too big and too tall, and the only thing that really stood out about him was his huge appetite and his concern for always getting to the feed-tub first.

Ben Castleman never liked to keep his colts and sold them as soon as possible. His fillies, however, he kept for racing and then breeding. So at the Keeneland Summer Sale Castleman asked the sale's agents to inspect his *Bold Reasoning-My Charmer* colt. They did, and they rejected him, saying that he simply did not look outstanding. They also felt that he would not sell because his sire and dam had not proved themselves as runners. Castleman's only alternative was to offer *Seattle Slew* at another sale, a bargain-basement one that Fasig-Tipton of New York had started the year before. He decided that if he couldn't get at least $15,000 for his horse he would race him himself. For two days dozens of people looked over the yearlings and most passed up the big, tall colt from White Horse Acres.

About 500 people attended the Fasig-Tipton auction at Lexington. This wasn't the company's blue-chip sale, which was to come in August at Saratoga, and few knew that this auction was to be taken seriously. The first such auction had taken place only the year before, and the horses from that sale had not yet shown their mettle. *Bold Forbes*, who had sold for $15,200, would win the Kentucky Derby and the Belmont, and *Elecutionist*, who had brought $15,000, would win the Preakness, but these results were still a year away.

When the *Bold Reasoning-My Charmer* colt was led in, very few people seemed to care. He passed by almost unnoticed and the bidders were few. Mickey and Karen Taylor of White Swan, Washington were among the small group bidding. The Taylors, each thirty years of age, were in their second year as thoroughbred owners. Mickey Taylor had been successful in logging and Karen had worked as a stewardess for North-West Orient Airlines.

They supplied the money for the thoroughbreds and relied on their silent partner, veterinarian Jim Hill, for the horse expertise. Hill felt the awkward colt had talent, and when the Taylors bid $17,500 for him he was theirs.

Initially, the Taylors and Hill planned to take all their two-year-olds to Sunland Park in New Mexico and make a fast return on their investment, but by September they had bought thirteen horses and there was room for only nine in the west. So the four with the least likelihood of developing quickly for the short two-year-old races in New Mexico stayed in the east. One of the four was *Seattle Slew*.

From the time he was sold as a yearling until he went into training the following February, *Seattle Slew* was in the care of Paula Turner at Andor Farm in Monkton, Maryland. She was an experienced horsewoman whose husband, Billy Turner, also enjoyed a fine reputation, first in the steeplechase and later as a top flats trainer. It was Paula Turner's job to break the colt whom she called ''Baby Huey'' because he reminded her of the overgrown cartoon duck. He required a good deal of patient handling, but learned his lessons well. By February he was galloping an easy three miles.

Paula then turned ''Huey'' over to her husband at Belmont Park in New York. Former steeplechase men who take up training runners usually come highly recommended, and Turner was no exception. The Turner stable trained and raced with the best.

Seattle Slew was to make his long-awaited racing debut at Saratoga in early August, 1976. He trained well for a tall colt, but did not appear exceptional until one morning when he was asked for speed. He showed so much power that Turner decided not to push him further for at least another month. The speed he showed came as a complete surprise; his looks were so deceptive. One morning at Saratoga he worked three-quarters of a mile in 1:10-1/5. But a setback took place when he hurt himself by wrenching a hock, and his training had to be halted for a month.

On September 20th *Seattle Slew* made his debut in a six-furlong race at Belmont Park for maiden two-year-olds. The morning-line was listed at 10–1, suggesting that few knew how fast he could run. His brilliant works at Saratoga were not carried in the Racing Form. Either fog upstate had made it impossible for the clockers to catch him, or, if they did know about him, they were keeping quiet for business reasons. When the betting on the race commenced, however, it was obvious that somebody knew something. The early favourite was *Seattle Slew* at 7–5.

The Taylors and Dr. Hill and his wife Sally now went to the paddock. *Seattle Slew* behaved well and didn't seem

to mind this new excitement. In the betting he was still the favourite, but at 5–2. The parade to the post was uneventful. Throughout the stands horsemen and horseplayers were puzzled that the betting was so heavy on the number ten horse, the big, tall unraced colt.

At the start, *Seattle Slew* broke badly, but quickly moved to the front and stayed there. He won by five lengths in 1:10-1/5, the same time he had taken for the six furlongs at Saratoga. The win was so impressive that after the race, Mickey Taylor and Jim Hill were offered $100,000 for him by an admiring trainer. Three days later the same trainer offered $300,000, but he was not for sale.

His next start was a seven-furlong allowance race on October 5th for non-winners of two, which he won easily by three and a half lengths as the heavy favourite at 2–5. Now, after just two races, both sprints, he was being pointed for the 105th running of the prestigious Champagne Stakes, the oldest two-year-old stakes race in America.

The ten-horse field in the Stakes included several seasoned and experienced horses: *For the Moment*, who had won the Belmont Futurity; *Ali Oop*, winner of the Sapling; *Turn of Coin*, winner of the Sanford; and *Sail to Rome*, winner of a division of the Cawdin. Despite the presence of these well-known horses, the crowd made *Seattle Slew* the 13–10 favourite. He drew the number three post position, raising the possibility of being trapped along the rail on the inside. His competitive ways and his desire to run could result in him literally climbing over any horse in front of him. Fortunately, there was no need for his owners to worry, for after one-quarter of a mile in the one-mile race *Seattle Slew* was in front. A quarter of a mile from the finish *For the Moment* moved up to him, but *Seattle Slew* drew away to win by nine and three-quarter lengths. The time for the mile was the fastest ever recorded for a two-year-old, 1:34-2/5.

The brilliant display in the Champagne Stakes made *Seattle Slew* the champion juvenile of America and the horse to beat in the three-year-old Classics. In less than one month he had created an incredible stir for a horse that had aroused so little interest when he was sold in Lexington the year before. People now wanted to see more of him. But the temptation to start in one more race, the Laurel Futurity in Maryland, was resisted, and he was taken out of training and given a rest.

At three, he continued to grow and to train well. Instead of spending a long cold winter in New York, he enjoyed the warmth and sunshine of Florida. So outstanding was he in the minds of the bettors that when he made his first start as a three-year-old he went off at 1–10. In the field at the seven-furlong allowance race at

Hialeah was one very fast rival, *White Rammer*, but *Seattle Slew* just ran away and hid. His time was a very quick 1:20-2/5.

This race was a prep for the rich Flamingo Stakes at nine furlongs where again *Seattle Slew* was the heavy favourite at 1–50. He did not let his backers down, winning easily. Oddly enough, some people were unimpressed by his performance because he did not maintain his initial huge lead.

A month later he returned north for the Wood Memorial in New York, the last big race before the Kentucky Derby. This nine-furlong effort turned out to be one more workout with a purse. Again there were those who thought he wasn't that good in the final eighth of a mile, but Turner thought it was a perfect race, especially since 'The Slew' had not started in a month. Besides, he had bigger races to win than the Wood Memorial at Aqueduct. There was the Triple Crown, and *Seattle Slew* was moving towards the first jewel.

On the first Saturday in May *Seattle Slew* was ready, and so was the huge crowd that packed historic old Churchill Downs for the Kentucky Derby. The track was fast and when the horses left the post the first announcement heard by everyone, including more than sixty million television viewers, was that "*Seattle Slew* broke slowly". However, in one of those famous split-second decisions so vital in sports, Jean Cruguet and *Seattle Slew* raced through the narrowest of openings with a burst of blistering speed to pass the stands alongside *For the Moment* after a quarter of a mile. Cruguet remained calm and stayed right beside *For the Moment* and Angel Cordero around the first turn and down the backstretch. *For the Moment* was on the inside, *Seattle Slew* on the outside. Then Cruguet eased back, just a length, until he saw *For the Moment* tiring. After that, it was no contest. *Seattle Slew* went right on by. Cruguet went to the whip, just hard enough to remind his horse of what they were both doing there. He increased his lead to three lengths in the long Churchill Downs stretch, and at the finish he was still ahead by almost two lengths, a comfortable and impressive win. Returning to the winner's circle he looked marvelous, with that magical aura that goes with being undefeated. Everyone was enthusiastic as the sports pages proclaimed, "'The Slew' Slayed 'Em."

The pressure was on, for it was only two weeks until the Preakness at Pimlico in Baltimore. The second jewel in the Triple Crown is never easy, but the track does suit speed, providing, of course, that a horse can take the lead early and maintain it. In the Preakness was the hero of Aqueduct's winter meeting, a fast horse called *Cormorant*. His fans said he could fly, but did not know how he would run against *Seattle Slew* in this, their first meeting.

This time, *Seattle Slew* did not get left at the post at the mile and three-sixteenths start. He sped away, but so did *Cormorant*. They raced as a team past the stands and into the turn. Cruguet did not need to urge his mount; *Seattle Slew* loved to run on this particular Pimlico track. Midway on the final turn he took off and won by a length and three-quarters. His mile was run in 1:34-4/5, the fastest mile in the history of the Preakness. The track had been made to order.

But the track was less than ideal three weeks later at New York's opulent Belmont Park, for the wind and the rain had come for the mile and a half Belmont Stakes. The anticipation was electric. The crowds had come to see a champion, to take part in an historical event. The tension mounted throughout the afternoon, especially when *Seattle Slew* was held up en route and arrived late. Cruguet, Turner, the Taylors and the Hills were all understandably on edge. A win or a loss in this particular Belmont could make a difference of millions of dollars.

After the first half-mile, 'The Slew' was relaxing in the lead. After a mile and a quarter the moment of truth arrived in the form of *Sanhedrin*, ridden by Jorge Velasquez. Cruguet called on his big horse to give it to him, and *Seattle Slew* started to pull away down the long Belmont stretch. He gave the thousands there what they had come to see, a Triple Crown winner, the first undefeated one in American racing.

All along, Billy Turner had planned on, and trained *Seattle Slew* for the Triple Crown. With this win, Turner was satisfied, but the great champion's owners were not. They wanted to see one more race, the rich Swaps Stakes at Hollywood Park. *Seattle Slew* finished far up the track, a pathetic looking fourth. *J.O. Tobin*, England's champion two-year-old, ran the race of his life to win with Bill Shoemaker by an incredible eight lengths.

Before the year was over, *Seattle Slew* was declared best three-year-old colt or gelding, and Horse of the Year. In nine of his ten races, he finished first and earned $735,720. Despite his obvious ability, *Seattle Slew* did not always enjoy a good press. Frequently during the height of his three-year-old Classic triumphs, more than one media man would say that he was the best of a poor lot. This, of course, was nonsense, for when he came back at four to race just a very few times, he was nothing short of astonishing.

Now trained by Douglas Peterson he ran an unforgettable race at rain-soaked, muddy Belmont Park in September, 1978. *Seattle Slew* ran away from *Affirmed*, the newest Triple Crown winner, but then *Exceller* with Bill Shoemaker came up along the inside to take the lead.

Seattle Slew came back inch by inch, only to run out of track right at the wire in one of racing's most desperately exciting finishes. *Exceller* was the winner, but both were champions. Only a rare kind of horse could share in the greatness of a race despite losing. *Seattle Slew* was just such a rare horse.

In 1978, his four-year-old year, *Seattle Slew* started seven times, won five, and finished second in two. He earned $473,006 for his owners, who now raced under the name of Tayhill Stable. It was a sign of how racing changed in the seventies that the Taylors and the Hills were subjected to an enormous amount of attention dur-

ing *Seattle Slew*'s years, as were their two trainers, Billy Turner and Douglas Peterson. They raced their champion with tremendous concern, then basked in the reflection of his brilliance.

Syndicated for $12,000,000, at $300,000 a share, *Seattle Slew* is one of the stallions at the famous Spendthrift Farm in Lexington, Kentucky. The questions about his offspring will soon be answered. All that can be said for certain is that it will be difficult for them to match the blinding speed at two, the Triple Crown at three and the great courage at four that gave American racing a star for three years, a star that shone brightly in the seventies.

Secretariat

became a household name while capturing America's first Triple Crown of the seventies.

Spectacular Bid,

a handsome grey powerhouse, became racing's first $22,000,000 champion.

Troy

won the 200th Epsom Derby by the greatest margin in over five decades.

Youth

triumphed in the French Derby at Chantilly and in the North American turf classics.

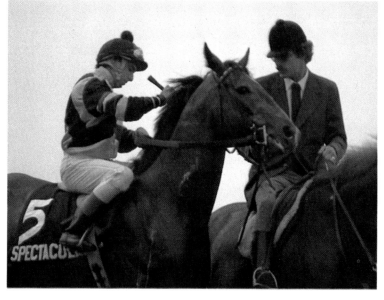

Secretariat

In his triumphant arrivals in the winner's circle, *Secretariat* had that aura of a champion which could bring smiles to winners and losers alike.

The scene was repeated so many times. In the circle were jockey Ronnie Turcotte, full of wonderment and admiration, Lucien Laurin, living a trainer's dream, and Penny Tweedy with the unlimited pride of the owner and breeder of a great horse. Around them thousands of people would applaud and cheer because for a few brief moments he was their champion too.

He still loves attention, and that is a good thing because he gets a great deal of it. Of all the stallions standing in Kentucky, *Secretariat* is the one that people from all over the world come to see.

He never disappoints them. When he suddenly moves at high speed in the paddock, his magnificent career is brought vividly to mind.

Spectacular Bid

On the racetrack *Spectacular Bid* is the kind of horse who trains as fast in the mornings as he runs in the afternoons. He closed out the seventies in the United States with a fine three-year-old year, and will open the eighties with a four-year-old campaign. It could well be that this sporting decision by the Meyerhoffs to go for the big handicaps will result in *Spectacular Bid* taking his rightful place among the greatest champions of racing.

Spectacular Bid

Spectacular Bid is a horse who prefers quiet. There is something about him in his stall that conveys his desire for complete privacy. His lack of concern for visitors and the curious makes them feel like intruders.

Unfortunately, no one was present when *'The Bid'* decided to pick at one of his protective stall-bandage safety pins. After managing to unpin it, he then succeeded in stepping on it. As bad luck would have it the small pin penetrated the sensitive laminae of the foot.

Fate decreed that the peculiar chain of events would take place in the early morning hours of Belmont Stakes Day.

Spectacular Bid lost the Belmont and the Triple Crown, and was lame the next day. With careful treatment and patient handling he returned to the races to prove he was a great champion of the seventies.

Troy

Troy's Derby was the last of the seventies.
No victory was more devastating than his triumph at
Epsom. In a smashing performance inside the final
two furlongs he ran away from the rest of his field
with every stride, winning finally by seven lengths.

Troy has always been a very quiet, placid horse.
His greatest admirers admit that he is lazy, but not
in his racing nor in his new duties as a stallion.

Triumphant on two continents

Youth won the French Derby, the Canadian International Championship and the Washington, D.C. International. He was invincible on soft, tiring ground.

His greatest victories were accomplished with ridiculous ease. He had a powerful style and made many moves that will not be forgotten.

His three-year-old campaign was a clever one. With a few brash performances *Youth*'s superiority was proved beyond any doubt.

Youth

Few horses have a chance to win their last race by such a commanding margin as ten lengths, but *Youth* did and he made it look easy. In 1976 he was the Best Grass Horse in North America.

He now stands at Gainesway Farm in the company of his former stable-mate *Exceller*. During the breeding season, Gainesway's stallion program operates like clockwork. As dawn is breaking, *Youth* is brushed and then, if he has an early engagement, he is taken to the breeding shed. Once his performance is completed, he is turned out into the paddock until his afternoon appointment.

It is during the period
that *Youth* is free to run
in his paddock that time
slips away, and he seems
like a young colt again.

Secretariat

At sixty years of age, after more than forty years in racing, starting as a jockey in Montreal in 1929, Lucien Laurin was about ready to retire to his Florida home for good. But as a trainer Laurin had never had a really great horse, and he suddenly found himself with the champion two-year-old of America. Meadow Stable's *Riva Ridge* was a horse too good to leave. He had a chance at the Triple Crown in his three-year-old-year in 1972. He almost made it, winning the Kentucky Derby and the Belmont Stakes.

With such a record in the books, it should have been easy for Laurin to take his bows and leave, but when the Triple Crown was still a dream Laurin had spotted talent in another Meadow Stable horse, a yearling sired by *Bold Ruler*. Owner Penny Tweedy had won the right to keep the colt by winning the toss of a coin with the sire's owner Ogden Mills Phipps, part of the deal by which Tweedy's mare *Somethingroyal* was bred for two seasons to the great *Bold Ruler*. The colt had impressed Laurin the moment he saw him, and while *Riva Ridge* was carrying his glory to the tracks on the west coast, in the east the colt was making his two-year-old debut.

It is fitting that the horse who would become one of the greatest in the history of American racing made his first start on the Fourth of July. The horse was *Secretariat* and the race was a five and a half-furlong sprint at New York's Aqueduct. Bumped badly at the start, he had to settle for fourth, the only time he ever finished out of the money. Eleven days later he was back again for a six-furlong effort and he won by six lengths. Moving on to Saratoga for two more six-furlong races, he showed once again that he loved what he had to do. In the first race on July 31st, he came home the winner by one and one half lengths. Then on August 16th he was tested in a stake, the Sanford Stakes, the same race in which *Upset* had beaten *Man o'War* in 1919. He left the gate in a rather unenergetic manner, but ran away to win by three lengths.

Maybe the memory of his first start down at Aqueduct stayed with him, for he never was that good away from the gate. He seemed to almost walk out, as if to say, "You go ahead, I'll be along later." The routine never cost him a race, and it probably helped him settle down for the big move later on. Jockey Ronnie Turcotte, who always marvelled at *Secretariat's* greatness, was the perfect rider to understand this style, because that's what it was–a style. There was no early speed duel, just a rather private start, a time to get organized, then a terrific run to obliterate the competition.

Turcotte maintained that just sitting up there on *Secretariat* was unusual. His great loins and hips were almost the width of two horses, a beam so broad that he had to have a special girth, and Turcotte said that when the time came to run, the sensation of acceleration was the same as one would get from a Cadillac. He could make an observer tingle with excitement. He had a beautiful way of going, with an enormous stride, truly the ground-devouring kind. He seemed to flow along, always perfection in itself, his head slightly down, nothing but smoothness and sizzling speed. And he was handsome, over sixteen hands, a beautiful looking chestnut with three white stockings. Big and muscular, he exuded strength and power.

Before leaving Saratoga, *Secretariat* started in the track's top race for two-year-olds, the well-named Hopeful Stakes at six and a half furlongs, and won handily by five lengths. Setting what was soon to be a familiar pattern, the saddling area was jammed with people trying to get a glimpse of the new Meadow Stable star.

For those speculating about the future, an important race was the 83rd running of the rich Futurity Stakes at Belmont Park on September 16th. *Riva Ridge* had won the Futurity the year before, and further back so had *Nashua*, *Native Dancer*, *Citation*, and *Man o' War*. The distance was again six and a half furlongs, and only seven horses went to the post, with *Secretariat* a heavy 1–5 favourite. At the start he was unhurried and didn't move until the field started to leave the turn. Then with a bold move he circled the leaders and quickly drew away to win by one and three-quarter lengths. *Secretariat* was beginning to command attention, though some still doubted his staying strength.

On October 14th he ran in his first distance race, the Champagne Stakes at one mile. It was the 101st running and proved to be memorable. Twelve horses made the long run down Belmont's backstretch and *Secretariat* was last until they had gone a half. Turcotte asked him to run and he started to circle his field while leaving the turn, but he could not keep a straight course and bore in on *Stop the Music* just inside the final three-sixteenths. Turcotte straightened him out by whipping him left-handed and he won in a driving finish by two lengths in 1:35 flat, but because of the interference the stewards reversed the order and *Stop the Music* became the official winner.

In two weeks he was in Maryland for the Laurel Futurity at one mile and a sixteenth, his first time around two turns. The track was sloppy. Only six horses were going for the $83,000 winner's purse, and the crowd made *Secretariat* a heavy 1–10 favourite. At the start he was unhurried, as usual, and Turcotte kept him well out on the outside. Leaving the backstretch he moved without urging, and when they turned for home he was going to the front. He won easily, finishing up by eight lengths with Turcotte sitting chilly.

He made his final start of the year a month later in the world's richest race for two-year-olds, the Garden State Stakes at Garden State in New Jersey, with a value to the winner of $179,199. *Secretariat* made it all look familiar. He was away sixth and last, moved around his field with his customary boldness, and then just bounded along in hand for Turcotte. His time for the mile and a sixteenth was 1:44-2/5, track fast.

The first horse to be both champion two-year-old colt or gelding and Horse of the Year in the same year, *Secretariat* was the cause of much speculation that was heavy and convincing. It wasn't only his record of seven wins in nine starts and his earnings of $454,404 that were impressive; it was the way he had won, with strength, speed and power. For those who had seen him there seemed to be

one conclusion – after twenty-five years American racing was going to see another winner of the Triple Crown.

This conclusion, of course, was only shared by people in the racing world, because the success of two-year-olds, even the most remarkable success, never gains the attention of the public at large. It is not really until the three-year-old Classics are up for renewal that those outside racing pay any attention, because only then does television turn its cameras on the sport to capture the feeling of the Triple Crown series. The glamour race of the three, the mile and a quarter Kentucky Derby at Churchill Downs in Louisville, Kentucky, is the one that almost everyone associates with the best in horseracing. Since 1875, when *Aristides* won the first Derby, the greatest champions in American racing have passed the old twin spires standing up from the roof of the grandstand of Churchill Downs.

There are legions of stories surrounding this historic race, many having to do with the million spent on trying to win it. But of greater interest is the training program for the horse. Horses mature greatly from two years to three, and a vital factor to consider for a serious Classic contender is how much racing and training he should have. Many stables prefer to take their horses to the winter sunshine of Florida, or the milder, but often wet weather of California, while others pass up these centres and remain in the North. Many Derby winners have been winter raced in the Flamingo at Hialeah or the Florida Derby at Gulfstream, in the Santa Anita and Hollywood Derbies in the west, or even in the rich races that take place in San Francisco, Hot Springs and New Orleans. The Meadow Stable of Penny Tweedy was sought after by every racetrack in the country. Everyone wanted to see *Secretariat*. But the decision was made to pass up the prizes at the traditional winter meets and stay in New York both for training and for a series of fine preps culminating in the rich nine-furlong Wood Memorial Stakes.

Secretariat made three starts, all of them at Aqueduct. The first was on St. Patrick's Day in the seven-furlong Bay Shore Stakes, where he carried scale weight of 126 pounds and won by four and a half lengths in the slop in the time of 1:23-1/5. The odds, as usual, were very low at 1–5. He made his second start in the one-mile Gotham on April 7th and won by three length in the sensational time of 1:33-2/5, equalling the track record. Even with 126 pounds on him he was such a handful that two lead ponies and an outrider were needed to pull him up. This strong finish added to the expectancy that at long last the Triple Crown would be claimed.

On April 21st he raced for the final time before the

Derby in the Wood Memorial Stakes. The picture taken in the winner's circle tells the story best. There, standing beside the $100,000 winner, is trainer Lucien Laurin looking as if he had been struck by some dreadful news. He had, for standing next to him is not a chestnut, but a bay. Even the owner of the horse, Ed Whittaker, and jockey Jacinto Vasquez appear to be in shock. The horse is *Angle Light*, who led the field all the way and held on to win over a black colt named *Sham*. Four lengths back was *Secretariat*. Because both horses were trained by Laurin, *Secretariat* and *Angle Light* were coupled in the betting, to the great relief of *Secretariat*'s backers.

Many reasons were put forward to explain the defeat, some thoughtful and others downright silly. Even when it was later revealed that *Secretariat* had suffered from a blood condition and an abcess on his lip, the theories still abounded. One of the most popular maintained that the *Bold Rulers* couldn't run a mile and a quarter. As so often happens in racing, just when some theory gains credibility and acceptance, a mighty force comes along to disprove it. In 1973, the mighty force was *Secretariat*.

His chief rival in the Derby was his Wood rival *Sham* with Laffit Pincay Jr. *Secretariat* closed in the betting at 3–2, the last time he would ever be such a price, while *Sham* was 5–2. In this 99th running at Churchill Downs, a field of thirteen broke from the gate and *Secretariat* broke last. As the solid wall of horses moved forward, each horse raising his own cloud of dust, *Secretariat* and Turcotte could be seen improving their position. When the field hit the first turn, Turcotte was already concerned with not dropping back too far. *Shecky Greene* was setting a fast pace and was well in the clear by almost two lengths. *Secretariat* gradually gained ground until the field hit the backstretch. Then, on the outside, easily visible with the naked eye, Turcotte's blue and white blocks of colours moved steadily ahead into seventh position, sixth position, fifth. *Shecky Greene* was slowing down in front and *Sham* and Pincay were right after him. *Secretariat* was increasing his speed. He had to, for *Sham* shot to the front in a big move that took him around the tiring leaders. When they turned into the stretch, it was *Sham* in front, with *Secretariat* driving up on the outside. Turcotte just showed him the whip on the left side, and he dashed into the lead to win by two and a half lengths.

Sham was game and held second by eight lengths over *Our Native*, who outfinished *Forego* for third, probably the best horse in years to finish out of the money. *Secretariat*'s run was a thrilling one, and when he came back to the winner's circle the crowd showed its approval. The Derby

had been run in new track record time of 1:59-2/5 for the mile and a quarter.

Two weeks later *Sham* came back, with four other horses, to oppose *Secretariat* in the Preakness Stakes at Pimlico in Baltimore, Maryland. The entire field broke smartly from the mile and three-sixteenths start, including *Secretariat*, for Pimlico is noted for favouring horses with speed, front runners, not early trailers or stretch runners. Its one-mile kite-shaped oval has a tight clubhouse turn, and the corners on it are sharp.

Ecole Etage led the way past the stands, followed by *Torsion*, *Deadly Dream*, *Sham*, who collided with *Deadly Dream*, *Our Native* and *Secretariat*. Most eyes were on the last horse. Turcotte eased him back, but he was travelling with more energy at this early stage than he had been two weeks ago at Louisville. He was also being eased to the outside as they went into the first turn. Once on the outside, still in last place, Turcotte gave him his head. *Secretariat* had never been asked to move this soon, but he loved it and roared past the field to take over the lead on the backstretch. He was never in danger from then on, simply speeding down the backstretch, rounding the far turn where he usually showed his boldness, then just for fun galloping through the stretch to Turcotte's super-confident hand ride.

Once again, *Sham* finished second after a game effort to chase the leader, and *Our Native* finished third. The Pimlico official time was 1:54-2/5, but the Daily Racing Form made it 1:53-2/5, a new track record. There were no more $5.00 payoffs; he returned only $2.60 to win. Two down, and one to go.

The pressure on Penny Tweedy, Lucien Laurin, and Ronnie Turcotte mounted. They were more than generous with both their time and their patience. Turcotte maintained through endless interviews, "He is the kindest horse I was ever around". Laurin marvelled at his enormous appetite and at his ability to relax. Penny Tweedy confirmed his intelligence when anyone was bold enough to wonder.

The day finally arrived, and as *Secretariat* walked from the barn to the stall awaiting him in the paddock a small army of admirers steadily gathered to follow him on his way. He looked like a champion, and what was strange, too, was that everyone wanted him to be a champion. Everyone wished Penny Tweedy well.

Five horses entered the gate for the 105th running of the Belmont Stakes. *Sham* was back, at 5–1, and there were three long shots, *Twice a Prince*, *My Gallant* and *Pvt. Smiles*. *Secretariat* was 1–10. At the start Pincay sent *Sham* to the lead, and Turcotte sent *Secretariat* right after him on the inside. After the first unbelievable fractions, the quarter in :23-3/5, the half in :46, the three-quarters in 1:09-4/5, *Secretariat* was in command. He had shaken *Sham*, while the others were another ten lengths back. Around the huge Belmont far turn, *Secretariat* opened up by seven, then ten, then fifteen lengths. The crowd roared its approval and disbelief. But as he came into the stretch, the astonishment grew, for he made his earlier running seem like a morning canter. The late Chic Anderson described it best by saying, "He is moving like a tremendous machine". Never has a horse run such a race.

Secretariat won the Belmont by an incredible thirty-one length margin in new track record time of 2:24. It was also a new American dirt course record for the mile and a half, and well it might have been the mile in 1:34-1/5, or the mile and a quarter in 1:59 flat. His greatness sent shivers through a crowd already joyous at having witnessed a feat not accomplished in twenty-five years.

The *Secretariat* story should, perhaps, have ended there, but it did not. "When's he going to run again?" It's a question that often tries the patience of trainers who, more than anyone, know the meaning of the old adage, "You run them often enough, then they'll get beat". *Secretariat's* next engagement was in Chicago on June 30th for the Arlington Invitational at a mile and an eighth. He won easily, staying on the crown of the track, by nine lengths in 1:47 flat, just 1/5 off the track record. Ronnie Turcotte always maintained that the race was harmful, because the track surface was very hard.

If it was it didn't show in *Secretariat's* training for the Whitney Stakes at Saratoga on August 4th, for in a workout he ran a mile in 1:34 flat, 4/5 faster than the track record. But, along with many horses, *Secretariat* then got the coughing virus and missed his Whitney blowout. The mile and an eighth race was his first try against older horses and *Onion*, a four-year-old, beat him by a length after he weakened in the stretch drive. Though he was 1–10 in the betting, he looked more like a defeated outsider when he came back in great distress.

He returned on September 15th in the inaugural running of the rich Marlboro Cup Handicap, an Invitational worth $150,000 to the winner. Seven runners started and into the stretch it was the two Meadow stars *Riva Ridge* and *Secretariat* in front, with *Secretariat* winning under brisk handling by three and a half lengths. The time of 1:45-2/5 was a new American and World record.

Two weeks later, Belmont was sloppy for the twentieth running of the Woodward Stakes at a mile and a half. Like the Whitney and the Marlboro, the Woodward was for older horses, and the result was another shocker,

especially after the Marlboro marvel. *Prove Out*, a four-year-old *Graustark* colt, loved the going and beat *Secretariat* by four and a half lengths. It was a difficult race to behold, for *Secretariat* seemed in command until *Prove Out* made his move. What made it even more incomprehensible was that only four days later, on October 3rd, *Secretariat* raced magnificently in Belmont's Man o'War Stakes. It was his final race with Ronnie Turcotte and his first start on the grass. Like the Woodward, it was at a mile and a half and he smashed the course record, getting the distance in 2:24-4/5. It was a powerful race, with Turcotte asking him twice to dispose of the good four-year-old grass champion *Tentam*, who finished second five lengths behind.

Secretariat had set a strange pattern in losing the Wood, the Whitney and the Woodward. An old track hand maintained, "He just didn't like them races beginning with a ' w '", but other opinions weren't so charitable. His training before these races was not as thorough as it could have been, but the three losing races became, in effect, part of the preparation for three of his four record-breaking races. The Wood was followed by the Kentucky Derby (a new track record), the Whitney by the Marlboro (a new American and World record), and the Woodward by the Man o'War (a new course record). Many *Secretariat* supporters felt he could have been undefeated, but "run them often enough, then they'll get beat".

Many supporters were also tremendously upset that his final race was in Toronto, not New York. There was an even greater disappointment for Ronnie Turcotte, who got a minor suspension of five days and had to miss a triumphant farewell in his native country. His friend Eddie Maple got the mount, while Turcotte had to look on. The preparation for the Canadian International Championship Stakes was unique. The Ontario Jockey Club management saw to it that the Woodbine grass course was trimmed to Penny Tweedy's specifications, and thousands turned out to see Turcotte and *Secretariat* in a final five-furlong work. Except when *Northern Dancer* returned from his Triple Crown series, no horse ever commanded such attention. His appearance made the mile and five-furlong Canadian International a truly World Class race.

In the excitement surrounding the occasion everyone overlooked that fact that the race would be run on Eastern Standard Time. It was 4:52 PM on October 28th, and the race was run in almost total darkness. The time had changed back from Daylight Saving Time that morning and everyone had overlooked the consequences. But nobody underestimated the moment of theatre as the race got underway. *Kennedy Road*, a Canadian champion home from greatness in California, made all the early running, but going down the backstretch *Secretariat* found him. They raced as a team to the start of the turn. From then on it was a question of how easily the American champion would win. On the turn he widened by twelve lengths, and maintained to the end a six and a half-length margin over *Big Spruce*, who was a length and a half in front of *Golden Don*.

The racing farewell for this extraordinary horse was an emotional experience. For some, it was simply a demonstration of greatness and not really a race. To this day, many people retain uncashed mutual tickets, programs, artist's prints, T-shirts, and other memorabilia of *Secretariat*'s magnificent career.

He was syndicated for $6,080,000 and stands at stud at Claiborne Farm in Paris, Kentucky. His yearlings have sold for world-record prices; *Canadian Bound*, who failed to win, brought $1,500,000. In 1978 his second crop came to the races and made him America's leading sire of two-year-olds. His best colt to race before the seventies ended was *General Assembly*, the Travers winner at Saratoga, and his best filly was the good *Terlingua*, a fast one on the west coast.

How well he will be remembered as a sire only time will tell. But as a racehorse his name will live as long as people thrill to the sight of horses running. *Secretariat* won sixteen of his twenty-one races and earned $1,316,808. He was America's Horse of the Year in 1972 and 1973. Perhaps he was the Horse of the Century.

Spectacular Bid

arry Meyerhoff of Hawksworth Farm had good reason to be on the lookout for horses sired by John W. Hane's stallion *Bold Bidder*, a son of the remarkable *Bold Ruler*. Not only had *Bold Bidder* sired the 1974 Kentucky Derby winner *Cannonade*, he had sired a filly named *Bold Place*. Meyerhoff had won over $100,000 with the filly before selling her as a broodmare for $250,000. So, when another son of *Bold Bidder* came up for auction, Meyerhoff, his wife Teresa and his son Tom decided to go after him.

The grey colt that caught their interest was foaled on Buck Pond Farm in Kentucky, the result of two Californians, Mrs. William Jason and her mother Mrs. William Gilmore, following the advice of bloodstock agent Vic Heerman to breed their mare *Spectacular* to *Bold Bidder*. Because *Spectacular*, a stakes-placed mare by *Promised Land*, had won less than $17,000 and because this was her first foal, the grey colt named *Spectacular Bid*, like *Seattle Slew*, wasn't considered good enough for the top yearling sales. He was offered, instead, at the Keeneland September sale. The Meyerhoffs were prepared to bid up to $50,000 for the grey, but they didn't have to go that high. In one of the best bargains ever seen at the Keeneland sale, they got him for $37,000.

Spectacular Bid was sent to the Middleburg, Virginia Training Centre to be broken by Barbara Graham, who considered him a good one right from the start. He also made a good first impression on the Hawksworth Farm trainer, Buddy Delp. A regular in the winner's circles of Maryland and New Jersey, Delp had saddled winners of more than two-hundred races a season for five years. While none had been top horses, many could really run.

Delp had proven he could spot a horse with promise, and he spotted talent in *Spectacular Bid* the first moment he saw him.

Spectacular Bid trained well over the Pimlico track in Baltimore and made his first start at the old Maryland track on June 30, 1978. In the five and a half-furlong sprint for maiden two-year-olds, he drew out to win by three and a quarter lengths, beating a good looking *Hoist The Flag* colt named *Strike Your Colours*. The time of 1:04-3/5 was only 2/5 off the record. It was an exciting performance, and produced a 6–1 payoff to the delight of his backers. He was still just another colt with promise, however, until he won his second start on July 22nd. At Pimlico, again at five and a half furlongs, apprentice jockey Ronnie Franklin made him run and he showed more than promise. He equalled the track record of 1:04-1/5 and won off by himself by eight lengths. Even the Pimlico punters were on to him, for he closed at 3–10. It was not only the win that excited his backers, but the way he won, because he showed he was learning well. He got the lead on the turn just when Franklin wanted him to, then easily proved that he was the best.

On August 2nd he started in another five and a half-furlong race, a division of the Tyro stakes at Monmouth Park. Over a sloppy track he started last, raced very wide, and finished ahead of some tiring horses, but still in fourth place. The Meyerhoffs and Delp were not discouraged, however, for he continued to train and act like a good one. Then, on August 20th, in Delaware Park's Dover Stakes at six furlongs, he broke with Franklin in reasonably good order, but not in what could be called a smart manner. At the half, Franklin waited too long and missed a possible chance to go on. The win was lost, though they finished second, two and a half lengths behind *Strike Your Colors*.

Fortunately, Franklin had an excellent working relationship with Bud Delp. He was a talented apprentice, learning all the time, and was actually a member of the Delp household, living with the trainer and his two sons, both of whom worked with their father. There was plenty of time to talk about racing, about the talented grey who was learning to run, and about how to correct mistakes such as the one that had lost the Dover Stakes.

By September 23rd, when he started in Atlantic City's seven-furlong World Playground Stakes, *Spectacular Bid* had learned to leave the gate better. He gave Franklin no problems as the young rider urged him on, and he moved between horses without trouble to get the first quarter in a quick 22 seconds. He opened up by two lengths after a half in :44-3/5, and by six lengths after six furlongs in 1:09. At the finish, *Spectacular Bid* was in front by fifteen lengths in 1:20-4/5, 2/5 off the track record. The whole performance was a driving one, and it proved he deserved a shot at New York.

Delp shipped him to Belmont Park for American racing's most important stake for two-year-olds, the one-mile Champagne Stakes. Only six horses faced the starter on October 8th, with *General Assembly*, a promising *Secretariat* colt, the 7–5 favourite off his Hopeful Stakes win at Saratoga. *Tim the Tiger*, the winner of the Sapling, was the second choice at 9–5, *Spectacular Bid* the third choice at 5–2. For this important race, Delp decided he needed all the jockey experience he could get, and engaged the veteran Jorge Velasquez, a regular New York rider.

At the start, *Breezing On* went to the front. *Spectacular Bid* stayed close to him along the inside, then went to the front with a rush leaving the backstretch, drawing away quickly, well out from the rail. *General Assembly* tried hard to stay with him, but couldn't do it. Through the stretch, *Spectacular Bid* continued on, passing the eighth pole with a four-length margin and winning under a good ride by Velasquez by two and three-quarter lengths in the exceptional time of 1:34-4/5.

Since 1940, when the Champagne distance was changed from six and a half furlongs to one mile, only three horses had ever run as fast, or ·faster in it than *Spectacular Bid*. *Count Fleet* also made it in 1:34-4/5 in 1942, *Vitriolic* did it in a sizzling 1:34-3/5 in 1967, and *Seattle Slew* managed the distance in a sensational 1:34-2/5 in 1976. *Spectacular Bid* was now being recognized as a top horse, but that wasn't good enough for the

Meyerhoffs or Delp. They knew they had a champion.

He made three more starts at two, all of them at a mile and a sixteenth, and each one at a different track. In the Meadowlands Young America Stakes on October 19th, Velasquez was on him again and had nothing but trouble at the start. It was a nine-horse field, and Velasquez had to overcome being badly shuffled back, which he did by moving boldly to the pace on the outside. On the turn, 'The Bid' advanced between horses, then gamely withstood the strong move of *Strike your Colors* through the stretch. He won by a neck. *Instrument Landing* was another neck back in third place in as good a finish as ever seen at the nighttime track.

Nine days later, with Ronnie Franklin back, he was at Laurel, Maryland for the Laurel Futurity. Only *General Assembly*, *Tim the Tiger* and *Clever Trick* opposed him. In the early stages he raced along with speed in hand, but *General Assembly* with Steve Cauthen came to him after five and a half furlongs. They drove hard at one another, but *General Assembly* could not keep up. In the stretch *Spectacular Bid* led by four lengths, and at the finish was in front by eight and a half in the new track record time of 1:41-3/5. He finished the season on November 11th by winning Keystone's Heritage Stakes with six lengths in hand. After seven wins in nine races (one second, one unplaced) and earnings of $384,484, he was named American racing's champion two-year-old.

With this brilliant record now in the books, *Spectacular Bid* was an obvious favourite for the 1979 Kentucky Derby and, for many, the Triple Crown. No one favoured him more than the Meyerhoffs and Delp, whose confidence in the colt was extreme. In fact, Delp declared that 'The Bid' could be the greatest horse of all time. Such statements were only part of the reason why the Hawksworth Farm group made news throughout the winter months. What is different is news, and *Spectacular Bid* and his young apprentice jockey Ron Franklin were different. Here was a colt commanding the entire racing world's attention for the rich three-year-old Classics, yet here also was a jockey with much to learn. Controversy, gossip and speculation abounded as *Spectacular Bid* went to Florida to start the 1979 season.

The first winter appearance was on February 7th in the seven-furlong Hucheson Stakes at Florida's Gulfstream Park. It was a fine beginning, with a win by three and three-quarter lengths in the good time of 1:21-2/5, just 3/5 off the track record. *Lot o' Gold* was second. Twelve days later *Spectacular Bid* finished first, eight and a half lengths in front of *Lot o' Gold* in the mile and a sixteenth Fountain of Youth. The win was in driving fashion, but, since horses are only as good as what they beat, it was noted that *Lot o' Gold* was, at best, fair.

The two met again on March 6th in the rich nine-furlong Florida Derby and, while the race dissipated some doubts about the horse, it raised the doubts about the rider to a new high. It was a race heaven-sent to the gossip mongers. *Spectacular Bid* got away badly, and Franklin seemed to panic. He rushed 'The Bid' up to the heels of horses and, worse still, into a pocket. He then made several moves which on a lesser horse would have meant certain defeat. But *Spectacular Bid* just continued to do what Franklin asked him to do. And what he asked him to do was run. He ran to the point where he was actually four horses wide, yet he still survived and drew off to win by four and a half lengths. *Lot o' Gold* was once again second.

There had been some serious risks taken with a tremendously valuable animal, already worth several millions, so the controversy heated up. There was relentless criticism in the press and on television. Though Franklin had been America's leading apprentice jockey in 1978 and had been honoured with an Eclipse Award, his lack of experience and poor judgement generated incredible hostility. It began to affect even his staunchest supporters—Bud Delp, whom he declared was like a second father to him, and the Meyerhoffs. At first, Delp was justifiably very upset over the Florida Derby ride, but he got over it, and the Hawksworth Farm group held firm. They did not fire Franklin, though many of American racing's top jockey agents continued to scratch their heads in wonderment.

Generally, most jockeys do not deserve the treatment some of them seem to get when they lose, and had Franklin been a veteran the controversy about his ride would have blown over in a few days. In fact, an experienced rider would probably have gotten away with, at worst, a mild rebuke. After all, there have been all kinds of races run by big horses with name jockeys up that have caused some alarm. The 1957 Kentucky Derby finish between *Iron Liege* with Bill Hartack and *Gallant Man* with Bill Shoemaker, for example, is legend because Shoemaker inexplicably and unbelievably stood up before the wire, raising the possibility that he didn't know where he was. Shoemaker lost the race. The great Lester Piggott couldn't find any room in the Washington, D.C. International on *Dahlia*, but it wasn't the end of the world and it certainly wasn't the end of Lester. And the Florida Derby ride wasn't the end of Franklin.

On March 24th, in the rich Flamingo Stakes, Hialeah's great nine-furlong winter Classic, Franklin was ordered to make 'The Bid' move. Taking no chances, Franklin rode him out in a devastating performance that saw him win by twelve lengths. While many horsemen dislike seeing their horses win by much more of a margin than they really have to, Delp knew that his big grey had to be ridden out, otherwise he might get the idea the racing business was just a game.

Another part of Delp's strategy was that 'The Bid' be given enough to do in order to be razor sharp for the five-week span that covers the Triple Crown. So he made one more start before the Kentucky Derby—the nine-furlong Blue Grass Stakes at Lexington's Keeneland Racetrack on April 26th. Only three horses showed up against him, including his old rival *Lot o' Gold*. *Spectacular Bid* was easily best and galloped home a seven-length winner. *Lot o' Gold* was a familiar second, *Bishop's Choice* third. Having now won ten in a row, *Spectacular Bid* was odds-on to win the world's most glamorous ten furlongs, the greatest two minutes in sports.

For the Kentucky Derby on May 5th, historic old Churchill Downs was jammed. The seventies had already seen three Triple Crown winners, so it wasn't enough now for the big grey to come through in the Derby; he was supposed to win them all. This was unprecedented pressure for anyone connected with a potential Classic champion, but the Hawksworth Farm people proved more than equal to it, handling the situation like experts. Ronnie Franklin, in particular, did his best, agreeing to what seemed like endless interviews, many of them springing from the premise of how it feels to be so green, yet have a chance win the Derby. Trainer Delp was steadfast, simply stating that *Spectacular Bid* was the greatest and that he would win.

The public agreed and made him 3–5. The second choice was *Flying Paster*, a California star who had pulled off a rich double by winning both the Santa Anita and Hollywood Derbies, third choice was *General Assembly*, and fourth was *Golden Act*, a horse good enough to win two 'hundred granders'. They were the toughest horses 'The Bid' had met since November, maybe ever. But when they were finally on their way it was more than obvious that they weren't too tough for *Spectacular Bid*.

On one of those cuppy, wet, but drying out tracks, 'The Bid' bounded along early in sixth place, not too close, not too far back. He stayed out, well out like *Forego* used to do, then one by one began to pick up the leaders. For a fleeting second he was with *Flying Paster*, then the Western invader had had enough. Franklin steered his mount up to the hard-running *General Assembly*, and they turned for home with the winner still in doubt. But *Spectacular*

Bid steadily and smoothly drew away and won driving by two and three-quarter lengths. *General Assembly* held on for second, and *Golden Act* was third. As always, emotions ran high both in the stands and the winner's circle, and Franklin won some well-deserved praise for a very fine ride.

There were no new challengers for *Spectacular Bid* in the Preakness at Baltimore's old Pimlico. The main threat once again was *General Assembly*, who was in excellent form and had good natural speed. But Delp was a Pimlico expert, and knew the surface of the kite-shaped track very well. He also knew *Spectacular Bid*, and gave him just the right amount of training designed to put speed into him so that he wouldn't be caught napping by *General Assembly*.

The training paid off. *General Assembly* was full of run, but so was *Spectacular Bid*. *General Assembly* and *Flying Paster* raced away together from the start. Franklin understood and waited. He waited until they reached the backstretch, then he moved from six lengths behind up to the leaders. *Screen King* with Angel Cordero Jr. forced him out much wider than he needed to be, but Franklin confidently continued on. As wide as any Classic winner had ever been, 'The Bid' came relentlessly on, as though losing ground did not matter. At the three-furlong mark on the turn he was in front. Turning for home he was in the clear by six lengths, then, still wide, he galloped through the stretch to win by five and a half lengths. *Golden Act* was second, *Screen King* third. The time was rapid, 1/5 off *Canonero II*'s track record of 1:54 flat for the mile and three-sixteenths.

The Hawksworth Farm group, all Marylanders, greatly enjoyed winning in their own backyard. Nobody now seemed to mind their unlimited confidence in the outstanding grey. Trainer Delp predicted that *Spectacular Bid* would become American racing's twelfth Triple Crown winner, and also declared, just for good measure, that 'The Bid' was up there with *Man o' War*, *Citation* and *Secretariat*.

But an unforeseen stroke of fate was to shatter Delp's dream and cause a sensation. During the morning of the Belmont, groom Moe Hall found a pin sticking into 'The Bid's' left front hoof, a pin that he had picked off his protective stall bandages. The pin was removed, and nobody said a thing. To the walking-ring observer, *Spectacular Bid* was more than on edge. At times he seemed almost over the edge. The confidence of Maryland was gone. Franklin, in particular, did not seem to be coping with the immediate task; he seemed terribly nervous. On parade, as the band struck up the familiar 'Sidewalks of New York', the Hawksworth group looked vulnerable.

For the first mile, *Spectacular Bid* looked like his old self. Franklin let him run, much in the tradition of other Belmont winners, for, surprisingly, horses that demonstrate speed most of the way, like *Affirmed*, *Seattle Slew*, *Secretariat* or little *Bold Forbes*, fare very well in this race. Then it happened. 'The Bid' was in trouble. *Coastal*, with a fine turn of speed on the inside, responded to Ruben Hernandez's urging and rushed into the lead. 'The Bid' couldn't catch him, nor could he hold second, giving way to *Golden Act*'s rush at the end. *Spectacular Bid* lost the Belmont by three and a half lengths.

The next day he was lame. The pin he had picked for fun had penetrated the very sensitive laminae of the foot, and the famous Kentucky veterinarian Dr. Alex Harthill expressed the opinion that the injury was a very serious one. He compared it with a finger nail injury to a human being, which can be extremely painful until the pressure is relieved from what seems like a small blood blister. 'The Bid' had greatly aggravated the situation by running in the Belmont, and, though the injury made the loss understandable, it did not make the disappointment of losing the Triple Crown any easier to bear.

The injury healed and he came back on August 26th in an allowance race at Delaware Park, but a familiar figure was missing. Delp had fired Ronnie Franklin and replaced him with Bill Shoemaker, the world's winningest jockey and one of the coolest to ever ride in a race. They won by seventeen lengths in new track record time on a track rated only good, and they triumphed again on September 8th in the $300,000 Marlboro Cup Handicap, winning the nine-furlong race by five lengths ridden out. This was sweet revenge, for *General Assembly* and *Coastal* finished second and third, while also up the track were *Cox's Ridge*, *Text* and *Star de Naskra*, all older veteran stakes winners. *Spectacular Bid* had done what *Seattle Slew* and *Affirmed* could not do at three–he had beaten older horses.

But the race everyone wanted to see was the mile and a half Jockey Club Gold Cup, because *Spectacular Bid* was finally meeting an older horse who was a true champion. *Affirmed*, now more developed and talented at four, had won six in a row, five of them stakes, including the Charles H. Strub Stakes, the Santa Anita Handicap, Hollywood's Californian, and the Gold Cup. And at Belmont, where he was readied for what was to be his final appearance, he had won the Woodward ridden out. *Spectacular Bid* had missed him in the Woodward because of a fever, and *Affirmed* had missed 'The Bid' in the Marlboro because trainer Laz Barrera thought 'The Bid' should have been assigned more weight. Now they were meeting at a mile and a half, a distance *Affirmed* had run the year before in a now famous Belmont with Alydar. Because *Spectacular Bid* had lost his Belmont, the Hawksworth group wanted badly to win, to somehow settle the score.

Affirmed broke smartly, 'The Bid' did not. The early pace was slow, with the first quarter in 25 seconds, but Pincay asked *Affirmed* to pick it up. Down the backstretch Shoemaker moved on 'The Bid' twice, but *Affirmed* just couldn't be caught. On the turn *Spectacular Bid* was dropping back little by little, while his Belmont conqueror *Coastal* was moving, coming between 'The Bid' and his pace-setting rival. Shoemaker maintained that at this point his mount spit out the bit, but on he came, battling back through the long Belmont stretch. He caught *Coastal*, but not *Affirmed*.

It was as game a race as any horse could run, for he had come on again and at equal weights had beaten his Belmont rival by three lengths. He just wasn't up to running down *Affirmed*, an older horse with so much natural speed, and strong staying power. He lost by only three-quarters of a length, and, while his bad start to *Affirmed*'s good start didn't help, excuses were not necessary. He put his Belmont into perspective. *Spectacular Bid* belonged at the top, running with the best in the world.

In his final start of 1979, the Meadowlands Cup Handicap, he drew away by three lengths and set another new track record for the mile and a quarter of 2:01-1/5. It brought his record for the year to ten wins in twelve races, with one second and one third. He earned $1,279,333 to bring his two-season total to $1,663,817.

Best of all, the terribly proud Meyerhoffs announced that he would continue in training and race at four. *Spectacular Bid* will be tested in the great handicaps, as *Seattle Slew* and *Affirmed* were tested. He will have to give away the weight to his rivals and still come through to win. Unless some star of true greatness emerges, the odds are that 1980 will belong to him.

Troy

The Gimcrack Stakes, first run at York in 1846, is one of England's most important races for two-year-olds. While the distance is only three-quarters of a mile, it was enough for *Mill Reef* to prove his potential when he won by an astonishing ten lengths in 1970, a performance that was the tip-off to a colt of rare quality. A horse named *Petingo* ran in the 1967 Gimcrack and went on to become a very good miler. When his racing was over he was bred to the *Hornbeam* mare *La Milo*, a filly more than capable at the middle distances of a mile and a half and thirteen furlongs. The dam with the stayer potential and the sire with the speed produced a middle distance champion rivalling Britain's best of the seventies. He was named *Troy*.

Sir Michael Sobell, one of England's leading philanthropists and benefactors, and his son-in-law Sir Arnold Weinstock raised *Troy* at their Ballymacoll Stud. *Troy* was the last of *La Milo*'s seven foals, all of them winners, including *Admetus* who triumphed over *Dahlia* in the 1974 Washington, D.C. International. Tragically, this grand producer had to be put down because of leg trouble after *Troy* was weaned.

Troy became a most impressive looking individual, very strong, the rare kind that can carry a good deal of weight. His celebrated trainer, Major Dick Hern, said he had everything: constitution, soundness, looks, and ability. But Hern observed that with every horse there is usually a weak link, and with *Troy* it was soft going; he just wasn't as good on it as on the firm.

In 1978, *Troy* made his first start as a two-year-old on June 28th carrying Sobell's pale blue and yellow colours across the course at Salisbury, the same course used by *Mill Reef* for his debut. The race was the Second Division of the Shrewton Maiden Stakes at six furlongs. It was a thirteen-runner field, and *Troy* went off as the favourite because of his good looks and good reports about his training. With two furlongs to go Willie Carson got him to the front, but he couldn't keep it up. *Nobloys* from France finished strongly, putting *Troy* away. Still, it was a good second, and it proved to be the tightener needed for the seven-furlong Plantation Maiden Stakes on July 11th at Newmarket. The going was good for the twenty runners and once again *Troy* was the favourite. He gave Carson a big run, and this time made it pay off, winning over *Warmington* by two lengths.

On July 27th at Goodwood in the Lanson Champagne Stakes at seven furlongs, five runners were out and all of them were winners. *Saracen Prince* with Lester Piggott led for the first five furlongs; *Troy* ran along last. When Carson asked him, *Troy* just streaked past his field to win over *Ela-Mana-Mou* by two and a half lengths.

His fourth and final start of the year was at Ascot in the one-mile Royal Lodge Stakes on September 30th. Into the straight, the favourite *Lyphard's Wish* had the lead and *Troy* was being hard-ridden by Carson just to keep up. They never gave up and finally caught the pacesetter with a furlong to go, but the effort had taken its toll, for *Ela-Mana-Mou* came on and caught them. *Troy* gamely held on, losing by three-quarters of a length. He now had a two-for-four record, good enough for *Troy* to finish in the top ten for his age.

The record wasn't enough, however, to generate any consensus about Classic victories at three, but this was only because *Troy* didn't have quite the same style as the other champions of the seventies. His style was deceptive. Willie Carson, one of *Troy*'s great admirers, has said with affection, "He was bloody horrible to ride, very lethargic. He didn't have instant speed, so he needed a distance to show his brilliance. He had to build up his speed, and settle into his own pace. He never took hold of the bit. He needed a strong pace for his best. He was a very quiet, placid horse to be around, and he never showed much until approaching the gallops. But then he'd try and run off with me. He's definitely the best I've ridden."

Troy started his three-year-old season with a victory in the mile and a quarter Classic Trial Stakes at Sandown in April. He beat *Two of Diamonds*, showing that he'd be a tough colt to deal with in the Classics. His second start was the Predominate Stakes at a mile and a half at Goodwood. *Troy* was being asked to go the Derby distance before the Derby. He found the added extra quarter of a mile very much to his liking. As they say in racing, 'He didn't beat much, but it was the way he did it.' His rivals were *Serge Lifar*, who had won only once, *Galaxy Libra*, who had also won once, and *No Evil*, a maiden who had been third once in her only two outings. They were a weak bunch compared with *Troy*, so it was little wonder that he led one furlong from home with a hand ride that resulted in a seven-length win at the wire. The seven-length win was an omen.

The 200th running of the Derby Stakes had all the pre-race form of a wide-open affair. Twenty-three runners went to the post for a record first prize of £153,980, and many had the credentials to make them top contenders. Three were undefeated as three-year-olds and had that marvellous aura that goes with always winning. One of these was the Queen's horse *Milford*, a son of *Mill Reef*, with the great Lester Piggott. He was the sentimental favourite with the hundreds of thousands who always have their flutter, but there was only one horse who had won at the distance, and that was *Troy*.

Lyphard's Wish made all the early running with a good fast pace, the kind that soon reveals who has the speed necessary to fall in behind the leader. *Troy* was one who didn't have the speed, but Carson kept after him to at least stay in the middle of the field instead of far back where he would be outrun and have too much ground to make up. On reaching Tattenham Corner, it was still *Lyphard's Wish*, with *Milford* second, then *Accomplice*, *Noelino*, *Northern Baby*, *Man of Vision* and *Dickens Hill*. *Troy* was tenth on the rail. Tenth and on the rail turning into the straight at Epsom means that if you're going to win, you'd better get out of there. Carson was forced to wait, but with two and a half furlongs to go he managed to find clear sailing on the far outside. *Lyphard's Wish* still led and half a dozen others were still fairly well placed, but *Troy* was running

on the far outside with such speed that the race would soon be his. With a furlong and a half to go he was in front by two lengths, and at the finish seven. *Dickens Hill* was second, and *Northern Baby*, a Canadian-bred *Northern Dancer*, was third.

Seven-length winning margins are so rare in the Classics, especially in a race like the Derby Stakes, that the effect is awesome. Not since 1925, when *Manna* won by seven lengths, had a horse been so superior. And *Troy* won going away with every stride; he had more, much more, so great was he on this day.

Since 1962, five English Derby winners, *Santa Clause*, *Nijinsky II*, *Grundy*, *The Minstrel* and *Shirley Heights* have added the first prize at the Irish Sweeps Derby at the Curragh to their winnings. In 1979, *Troy* joined this select group. With only nine runners over a course rated firm, *Troy*'s uncelebrated stable companion *Rivadon* was the pacemaker. He opened up a huge lead, but got tired before the straight when *The Bart* took over. Into the straight, *The Bart* was well clear over *Fabulous Dancer*, *Scorpio* and *Troy*, but *Troy* was now making his familiar move, a long run that carried him to the front halfway through the straight. He never weakened from the effort and continued to run as fast as he could, winning by an easy four lengths. It was impressive, and there was now no doubt about *Troy* being something special. The Epsom rivals that he had put away with such ease raced well on many a racecourse after Derby Day, so it was difficult to dismiss *Troy* as one who had not beaten much. And the manner in which he did his racing, with a strong, powerful long run, set him well above many strong three-year-old rivals.

Against older horses he was still untested until Ascot's King George VI and Queen Elizabeth Diamond Stakes. He went off as the favourite because he had already won at the King George VI distance of a mile and a half three times out of three. The seven runners set a slow early pace not to *Troy*'s liking, but he managed under Carson's urging to get on with his race and assumed complete control once he was on his way. *Troy* won from *Gay Mecene*, a four-year-old winner from Saint-Cloud, by a length and a half. *Ela-Mana-Mou* was three lengths back in third. *Troy*'s triumph at Ascot was very predictable, especially since missing from the field were many fine horses including *Ile de Bourbon*, *Top Ville* and *Le Marmot*. He lived up to his notices, but not with the brilliance of *Nijinsky II* in 1970. A horse cannot be awesome every time, especially when the opposition is not, and with tougher runners and a quicker pace *Troy* might have been forced to be brilliant. But brilliant or not, he had now won a most prestigious treble of Classic mile and a half races. Only *Nijinsky II* , *Grundy* and *The Minstrel* had done it before.

Happily for racegoers, *Troy*'s connections were keen to have him do more, and after several races were considered, two were selected to complete the three-year-old year: the Benson and Hedges Gold Cup at York and the Prix de l'Arc de Triomphe at Longchamp.

The Benson and Hedges, at ten and a half furlongs, was one and a half furlongs shorter than *Troy*'s last four races. Such a change makes a race more difficult, as a rule, than it would be if a horse was coming off a ten-furlong race since it is easier on a horse to go from shorter distances to longer. And *Troy*'s competition included *Crimson Beau*, off a good Ascot win, and *Lyphard's Wish*, who had led the way at Epsom for a mile and a quarter.

The rich York meeting has a history of shocking upsets, and three furlongs from home another reversal seemed likely. *Lyphard's Wish* and *Crimson Beau* were strong leaders, and *Troy* looked desperate. He had been hard-ridden just to keep in range, and now was about twelve lengths back. The situation was different from his four middle distance victories, because in those races Carson hadn't had to use him much in the early running. The ten and a half furlongs of dead ground was also tiring, and *Troy* loved the going to be firm with a good bounce to it. But Carson finally got him going for a ground-devouring run that brought him to the front with little left to spare. Carson let up on him in the final yards, resulting in a three-quarter-length margin over *Crimson Beau*, with *Lyphard's Wish* four lengths back in third. The long desperate run was a moving sight, and to *Troy*'s talents already in abundance could now be added great courage and gameness.

There was much anticipation surrounding *Troy*'s start in the Prix de l'Arc de Triomphe. Not since *Nijinsky II* in 1970 was there so much hope for an English- and Irish-raced horse to win at Longchamp. *Troy* was the undisputed odds-on favourite, but the ground again was not to his liking and his season had been a long one, with some very demanding moments at York. *Troy* met the best in Europe on the first Sunday in October on a day that brought out the sun, the President of France and a vast throng, including thousands of British supporters. The field included a strong trio of middle distance runners, *Top Ville*, *Le Marmot* and *Ile de Bourbon*, each very dangerous at the distance. *Le Marmot* was reported to be razor sharp. There was also *Three Troikas*, a *Northern Dancer* granddaughter by *Lyphard*, who had won six of her seven races.

Twenty-three runners went to the post. Into the straight, with about two and a half furlongs to go, *Troy* and Carson were well positioned, about tenth, not too far back. *Northern Baby*, always dangerous at a mile and a quarter, took over, but not for long because *Le Marmot* was challenging and gaining the upper hand. *Troy* was moving, but not with great power. The horse with the strength was the filly *Three Troikas* who was cutting down *Le Marmot*'s lead. Inside the final furlong there was no doubt that *Three Troikas* was going to do it, and she did, with a convincing three-length margin over *Le Marmot*, who ran gamely to hold second. *Troy* finished third. In North America it would have been said that *Troy* failed to fire; months later Carson simply said he couldn't find the accelerator. On Prix de l'Arc Day a horse must be at its best, and while *Troy* looked at his best and, until the serious running, seemed at his best, his Arc at Longchamp was far below his Derby at Epsom.

Troy was retired to Highclere Stud, Newbury in the Berkshires. He was syndicated for a record £7,200,000 before his defeat in Paris, but his record was always on the line. And the record speaks for itself: eleven starts, eight wins, two seconds and a third. His winnings totalled £450,494.

His conversion from a superbly trained, highly accomplished racehorse to a stallion took place without incident, for his temperament made him easy to work with. Although, as in his races, his docile nature often shows itself as laziness, he is wonderfully reliable in the breeding shed where, it is hoped, he will pass on those qualities of a champion that he so generously displayed. He was a marvellous horse to end the seventies, for he gave English racing a home-bred to round off a decade that had begun with *Nijinsky II* and *Mill Reef*, and continued with *Grundy*, *The Minstrel* and *Alleged*. It was one of the finest decades in English racing, a decade of champions.

Youth

The Prix de Diane, the French Oaks, at one mile and five-sixteenths, is one of the world's richest races for three-year-old fillies. Run each year in June at beautiful Chantilly, the Oaks first money is now worth up to $207,000. It has built up a wonderful tradition since the first running in 1843, and through the years many of its winners have made racing history. The great American-bred 'French' fillies *Allez France* and *Dahlia*, for example, finished one-two in the Oaks in 1973. But for sheer theatre *Gazala II*'s finish in 1967 was surely the most dramatic. With only one furlong to go she was absolutely last, racing twenty-third in a field of twenty-three horses, and she won. She won with a fantastic finish that is still discussed with admiration and awe.

Gazala II came by her ability to be astonishing quite honestly, for her sire was *Dark Star*, the horse that Captain Harry F. Guggenheim got lucky with in the 1953 Kentucky Derby. The heavy favourite in the Derby that year was Alfred G. Vanderbilt's undefeated grey *Native Dancer*, who had developed into a devastating stretch-runner. *Dark Star*'s jockey, Henry Moreno, was instructed to try his best to 'save' his mount for when it would really count, but, luckily for him, things did not work out that way. *Dark Star* broke from the gate so full of run that Moreno simply could not restrain him. He vaulted into the lead and stayed there. Big *Native Dancer* with Eric Guerin up was knocked about badly by *Money Broker* and Al Popara into the turn and never recovered completely. For the longest time he failed to respond to Guerin's whip, which was being used for the very first time, and when he finally got going it was too late. He couldn't catch *Dark Star*, who won by a head. *Gazala II*'s sire had pulled off one of the most astonishing surprises of all. It was the only time in twenty-two starts that *Native Dancer* lost.

Guggenheim had another memorable horse in *Ack Ack*, though unfortunately he never lived to see this one's greatness. *Ack Ack* came in first or second twenty-five times in twenty-seven starts, and when he won the ten-furlong Hollywood Gold Cup carrying 134 pounds, he made such a task look easy. His strength was speed, and Nelson Bunker Hunt made the decision to breed *Gazala II* to him. The result was a bay colt named *Youth*.

Gazala II had distinguished herself early by producing a top French colt named *Mississipian*, sired by the famous Arc winner *Vaguely Noble*. So *Youth* was a half-brother to a colt with class. He was a strong looking colt, though too long in the back, perhaps more tough looking than good looking. He always showed good acceleration, not surprisingly when one remembers his mother's startling late speed. As a two-year-old he left the fields of his Maryland farm and joined two other promising Hunt colts, *Empery* and *Exceller*, in the famous yard of Maurice Zilber, one of French racing's canniest trainers.

Zilber soon recognized the tell-tale signs of precociousness so essential for a Classic prospect. The French often feel that if a horse has talent it is better to wait and let him develop so his strength is there when it counts. *Youth* was, therefore, raced very sparingly at two. He was a winner first out at Longchamp in September, and came back with a good second in October. Two starts showing good potential were enough for Zilber. He put *Youth* away for the next year.

Youth matured greatly in 1976, and trained superbly for Zilber, doing everything he was asked to do. His main objective was the Prix du Jockey Club, the French Derby at Chantilly in early June. With this objective in mind, a training schedule was devised to include a number of races designed to bring him along. The program Zilber followed consisted of three pre-Derby races, each one of them an important Classic trial. All were at Longchamp and all were at the same distance, one mile and five-sixteenths.

Youth made his three-year-old debut on April 4th with Freddy Head in the saddle. The going was slow, but he made a strong finish and won by a length and a half. It was a good effort, but certainly not one he managed with speed to spare. Neither *Velino* nor *Yule Log*, who were two-three behind him, had been a pushover in the running. On April 19th he made his second start and already showed great improvement. The going was good, and Freddy Head got a fine response when he asked for it. *Youth* led the field for the final two furlongs and won by four lengths over *Danestic* and *French Scandal*. In the last and most important Classic trial, the Prix Lupin on May 16th with a winner's purse of just over $100,000, the going was again good and Head kept *Youth* well up when it counted. He took the lead just when Head wanted him to and held on smartly over both *Arctic Tern* and *Youth*'s much improved stablemate, *Empery*.

On the basis of the Prix Lupin result, Zilber and Hunt made the decision to start *Empery* in the English Derby, while keeping *Youth* for the French. *Empery* seemed more a stayer than *Youth*, more the right type of horse for the Epsom course. If both horses managed to win, it would be a rare double not seen since Marcel Boussac's *Galcador* and *Scratch II* accomplished the same feat in 1950.

Empery's third place finish in the Prix Lupin was also encouraging enough for Lester Piggott to take the mount on him for Piggott's twenty-third Derby ride. Up to now, six of these rides had led to victory. *Empery* was up against some very good horses, including *Vitiges* and *Wollow*, the latest to be labelled 'wonder horse'. But on the first Wednesday in June, these two failed to live up to their notices. *Empery* took the Derby by three lengths.

Four days later, in the French Derby at Chantilly, Freddy Head kept *Youth* never worse than fifth during the early running. He moved strongly to the lead at the ten-furlong marker, then ran like a demon the last quarter. The race was a fast one and he won by three lengths without any strong challenge. *Twig Moss* was second, *Malacate* third, *Granshaut* a disappointing fifth after a run full of trouble, and *Arctic Tern* was well back in ninth. What a week in racing for Bunker Hunt and Maurice Zilber! The stablemates had come through in tremendous fashion. Of the two, *Youth* certainly seemed the best, and

this was confirmed when *Malacate* went off to the Curragh to beat *Empery* in the rich Irish Sweeps Derby.

Before June was over both the Hunt horses were sold for $6,000,000. Twenty members of a syndicate contracted to pay $300,000 for a share in both. The two were to be retired to stud at Gainesway Farm at Lexington, Kentucky at the end of their three-year-old years. For each share, a syndicate member was entitled to a service to each horse. To the chagrin of some, and the horror of others, *Empery* never did win again. After failing to fulfill his post-Irish Derby engagements, *Empery* was retired.

Youth also had a shock in store for his supporters, and he delivered it on July 24th. The race was the ten-runner King George VI and Queen Elizabeth Diamond Stakes at Ascot. *Youth* beat one horse to finish ninth, eleven lengths behind the winner *Pawneese* with Yves Saint-Martin. *Bruni* and *Orange Bay* finished second and third. *Youth*'s weakness came as a big surprise, particularly when contrasted with his strong stretch strength at Chantilly, and caused both wonder and consternation. Perhaps the poor showing was because of the footing. The ground at Ascot was firm, and this was a course condition *Youth* had never experienced. Perhaps coincidental, but the fact remains that the only time *Youth* ever ran on firm turf he lost. There was also jockey Freddy Head whose Longchamp and Chantilly rides were legend for brilliance, but who had never been noted for finesse and good judgement at either Ascot or Epsom. His King George ride did not disturb this notion. Then again, perhaps *Youth* simply didn't like England. It was his first trip there, and he never returned.

Lester Piggott had the mount the next time *Youth* ran, which was at Longchamp on September 5th in the Prix Niel. The going was good for the mile and three furlongs and Piggott got the best of his four rivals from the start. *Youth* led the whole way, except for a brief time when he permitted *Loosen Up* to head him. *Arctic Tern* finished second, *Malacate* third. *Youth* won going away, by no means with ridiculous ease, but with enough style and strength that he was a co-favourite with *Exceller* at 2 – 1 in the Prix de L'Arc de Triomphe.

For this richest race on the European calendar, twenty runners took to the course on October 30th. Piggott this time chose to ride *Bruni*, the good four-year-old *Sea Hawk* colt who had won the 1975 St. Leger. Bill Pyers got the mount on *Youth* and must have wondered about Piggott's handicapping. Pyers rode perfectly, staying third behind *Pawneese* and *Kasteel*, then moving into the lead soon after the turn. For a brief moment it looked like *Youth* would make it, but first came *Ivanjica*, then *Crow*. *Youth*'s losing margin was five lengths, but he wasn't disgraced, for he held third gamely against the best of the remainder. It wasn't exactly a grand finale, but it was a finale, nevertheless. *Youth* now left France for good and was shipped to Canada on his way home to the U.S. .

The Canadian stop was in Toronto for the Canadian International Championship Stakes. Having seen the Internationalists *Dahlia* and *Snow Knight* the two previous years, Toronto now welcomed the hero of the French Derby. To ride *Youth*, Zilber engaged Canada's champion jockey Sandy Hawley, who had ridden an incredible 515 winners in North America in 1973 and who was the darling of Toronto racegoers. *Youth* and Hawley made for a powerful combination at slightly below even. The course was soft and tiring, but *Youth* loved it. In the first half of the mile and five-furlong race, Hawley kept him well back. *Crackle, Detrimental* and *Kamaraan II* , a French horse, made all the early running and then tired badly. The strong American invader *Effervescing*, who hated the going, tried to get into contention along with another American, *Improviser*, but it was all in vain. Hawley moved *Youth* when the leaders tired, a timing that resulted in *Youth* looking as strong as any horse had ever been, and then he simply galloped through the stretch to win by as much as Hawley pleased. *Improviser* was second, *Effervescing* third. The win made Hunt and Zilber two for two in the Canadian International Championship.

Still following in *Dahlia*'s hoof-prints, Zilber, Hawley and *Youth* moved on to the final stop before the breeding shed at Gainesway, the Laurel Racecourse at Laurel, Maryland for the mile and a half Washington, D.C. International. It was the 25th running of this rich race, which had been international from its inaugural running, a dream realized by its promotor, John Shapiro. First won in 1952 by the English runner *Wilwyn*, the International had seen many greats, including *Kelso*, who lost three years in a row before finally beating *Gun Bow* in 1964,

Match II , Daitome, Behistoun, Sir Ivor, Dahlia, Admetus and *Nobiliary*. In this running the eight-horse field included *Ivanjica*, the hero of the Arc, who was a co-favourite in the betting with *Youth* at 9–5.

As in Toronto, the ground was soft and tiring, conditions favouring a very fit horse that can handle the going. Riding a waiting race over such a course is almost mandatory, unless the horse is the speed type that simply cannot be rated. *Youth*'s fitness was in question right up to the morning of the race, however, for he had cut his off-hind heel earlier and its response to treatment had been a little slow. But he was passed by Zilber and his veterinarian, and left no doubt that he was fit to run.

Under Hawley's hands he was encouraged to go for a furlong to get a good position, then he remained wrapped-up until the mile. At this point he accelerated as only he could do and raced past both *Ivanjica* and *On My Way II* . When almost clear he crossed over to the rail sharply, a sudden swerve that caused some interference to *On My Way II* . But once straightened out with some hard left-handed whipping *Youth* simply ran away. He won by ten lengths. *On My Way II* was second, and the Arc rival *Ivanjica* finished third, narrowly losing second on the wire. The ten-length margin was a blessing for *Youth*. Had it been a closer finish the stewards might have ruled that interference had cost *On My Way II* the race, but the margin was more than convincing. *Youth* was named best grass horse in America.

It was a happy day for Hunt and Zilber. *Youth*, unlike *Empery*, went out in style. He had raced eleven times and had earned $687,644. He had finished first in eight of those races because of an acceleration that was unforgettable. When his two-year old colts come to the races in 1980 it wouldn't be surprising to see some of them, too, move suddenly with a boldness that might startle or astonish. That's the way *Youth* and *Gazala II* both did it – with a speed that is the mark of champions.

Epilogue

The nineteen seventies were remarkable years in the long history of thoroughbred racing. Many factors conspired to make the decade memorable and unique.

On the most public level, one feature of the decade was that the mass media, particularly television, focused on racing as never before and made the best horses stars. Few people in North America can now avoid hearing about horses during the five weeks from the first Saturday in May to the second Saturday in June. Awareness of the Derby, the Preakness and the Belmont can't be escaped. *Secretariat, Seattle Slew, Affirmed* and *Spectacular Bid* ran into millions of lives on Saturday afternoons, and their names became synonymous with the best. And in Europe *Nijinsky II*, *Mill Reef, Grundy, Red Rum, Alleged, The Minstrel* and *Troy* all became heroes via TV.

That some of the horses who gained fame in Europe were bred on the other side of the Atlantic points to another feature of the seventies: the growth of international racing. Bigger purses, highly competitive racetrack management and more efficient air transportation all contributed to this growth, as did the desire of many racing people to see their colours carried to victory in another land. *Nijinsky II* and *Mill Reef*, for example, raced in Europe because their American owners simply loved European racing. And the exploits of these two champions early in the decade convinced Europeans that there must be more where they came from.

The Minstrel and *Alleged* were bought in North America by syndicates controlled in Britain. They raced in Europe, then when their racing was done they returned to North America to stand at stud. *Dahlia, Youth* and *Exceller*, all American-owned, were raised in the U.S. , were trained in Europe, raced in Europe, then raced in North America before being retired.

Transatlantic travel was not restricted to the horses in the seventies, either. Ideas travelled as well. The European method of racing potential champions with great care as two-year-olds was not only at long last better understood in North America, but was beginning to be put into practice. And the enormous strength and durability of North American-raced horses was put into perspective by the understanding of the tremendous pressure put on them with their continual racing and travel over vast distances.

Knowledge about the greatness of particular races also travelled well. North Americans began to appreciate the Derby Stakes at Epsom and the Prix de l'Arc de Triomphe, while Europeans came to know more about the American Triple Crown series. The races became known because the horses made news. Much of the news centred on money.

The seventies was a decade marked by inflation everywhere, but in the world of thoroughbred racing and breeding it was a decade of incredible inflation, with world-record yearling prices, world-record stallion syndication prices and record prizes for races. By the end of the decade the sums involved were becoming astronomical. *Spectacular Bid*, sold as a yearling for $37,000, was working on his third million in prize money as a racehorse in

1980 and was already syndicated as a stallion for $22,000,000. In the seventies money seemed to be no object in the quest for a champion.

And the champions abounded during the decade, right from the first year when the English Triple Crown was won for the first time in thirty-five years. In the U.S., where a Triple Crown winner had not been seen for a quarter of a century, the Crown was claimed three times within the short space of six years. It was this abundance of remarkable horses that really set the decade apart.

While the profusion of champions delighted race-goers, it was in many ways a puzzling phenomenon, particularly the appearance of three Triple Crown winners when there had been none for so long. Many reasons were advanced to explain it, but none completely satisfied.

Many breeders maintained that the phenomenon was the result of better breeding, others thought it all due to chance. Some horsemen closer to the training of thoroughbreds figured it was because fields, particularly in Triple Crown races, were smaller. A few people thought the reason was that two-year-olds were being brought along more slowly. Some even said that the answer lay in air transportation replacing the slower and more weary-ing shipping by rail. But Alfred G. Vanderbilt, a leading American owner-breeder, probably said it best when he remarked, "I don't know how you can explain it. You get two horses back to back. There's no reason. It just happens."

While there may be no consensus on why so many champions appeared in the seventies, there can at least be some agreement as to what a champion is and what qualities one must have.

Champions have to win. They also have to lose, for only the rarest of thoroughbreds escapes defeat at one time or another, but it is amazing just how often they do avoid defeat. Champions must have speed and stamina; for these qualities there are no substitutes. But champions must also have heart and courage, for these combine to win the day when another horse with equal speed and stamina suddenly challenges. When a horse is proclaimed to be 'all heart', he is receiving the highest praise a racing enthusiast can offer, because champions are made when they are forced to the limit and still come through to win.

Champions usually have good people, too. Care and patience, good management and handling all contribute to a horse's performance, but more than one horse has made a great trainer or the reputation of a jockey.

Above all, champions have one special quality that sets them above the merely excellent, and that is the quality of *class*. They beat the best, they beat them often, in their own particular style – in front, just off-the-pace, or from far behind. They win with equal weights at three, then with higher and top weights at four and older. They win at whatever the distance and over whatever the going. No matter the demands put upon them, they show greatness in performance.

Which horses show these qualities enough to be called champions? One person's list could never be another's, and the differences of opinion traditional in racing are sure to be even keener than usual when discussion turns to a decade like the seventies when so many great ones appeared on the scene.

So it is worth reviewing why the seventeen champions profiled here were selected above others who could well lay legitimate claim to the title.

The big Canadian horse *Nijinsky II*, *Northern Dancer*'s greatest son, started the seventies off with a sensational sweep of England's historic Triple Crown, the first horse to do so since the Aga Khan's unbeaten *Bahram* in 1935. He was undefeated in his first eleven races, including five world Classics.

Beautiful *Mill Reef*, the brilliant bay son of *Never Bend*, had great natural speed and marvellous stamina. A Derby Stakes winner, he won the day for England with a devas-tating run at Longchamp. A colt of great courage, he survived a near-tragic end to become a leading sire at Newmarket's National Stud.

Secretariat, the striking *Bold Ruler* chestnut, did more for racing than anything in memory with his Triple Crown series. At a time when Americans were going through many difficulties, *Secretariat*'s phenomenal dis-plays of power replaced frowns with smiles. His devastat-ing Belmont Stakes victory by thirty-one lengths was a performance almost impossible to imagine. He was the darling of American racing and the first Triple Crown winner since *Citation* in 1948. For many *Secretariat* was not only the American Horse of the Decade, but also the Horse of the Century.

Dahlia, the chestnut daughter of *Vaguely Noble*, was one of the great fillies of the seventies, a winner on both sides of the Atlantic. Bred in Kentucky, she learned to run in France, and achieved her greatest feats at England's Ascot, where she was a repeat winner of the King George VI and Queen Elizabeth Stakes. She was a filly of rare stamina.

Allez France, the great bay daughter of *Sea-Bird*, was the only filly of the decade who could compare to *Dahlia*;

indeed, in each of their meetings, she finished ahead of *Dahlia. Allez France* failed to win when she travelled to England and America, but on her home ground she was the Queen of Longchamp. Her perfect season of 1974 when she was undefeated in five starts had no finer climax than her desperate victory in the Prix de l'Arc de Triomphe.

Grundy, the chestnut colt by *Great Nephew,* cost only 11,000 guineas because most buyers dismissed him as too flashy and not fashionable enough in his breeding. But he was Britain's champion colt of 1975 when he won the Derby Stakes, the Irish Sweeps Derby, and the King George VI and Queen Elizabeth Diamond Stakes in record time.

Red Rum, a small Irish-bred by *Quorum,* won some modest races on the flat at two and three, then learned to jump over hurdles. With a succession of trainers and jockeys he raced unnoticed year after year, until he was trained on the sands at Southport. Then for five years from 1973 to 1977 *Red Rum* was the 'King of Aintree', the undisputed champion steeplechase horse of Britain, a three-time winner of the great Grand National.

Mighty *Forego,* the huge gelded bay son of *Forli,* won three consecutive Eclipse Awards as America's Horse of the Year. His relentless stretch charges were the talk of New York racegoers. His tremendous burdens of weight made him the top weight-carrier of the decade. He was always handicapped, yet no matter how high the weight, he came through in the stretch. He won an incredible thirty-four races over six seasons.

Youth, a lightly raced bay son of the speedy *Ack Ack,* made only eleven starts, nine of them at three in 1976. But he won the Prix du Jockey Club, the French Derby at Chantilly, the Canadian International Stakes at Toronto's Woodbine, and the Washington, D.C. International Stakes at Laurel, all of them in superb style.

Exceller, a bay son of *Vaguely Noble,* raced in France, England, Canada and the United States. His seasons spanned half a decade, but no year was as good as 1978 when he won seven out of ten, even beating the mighty *Seattle Slew* in a memorable battle that can never be ignored. No horse ever travelled faster than *Exceller* on Belmont's big muddy turn for home. A winner of eleven Group 1 races, Exceller was the most under-rated horse of the decade.

The Minstrel was the second son of *Northern Dancer* to win the Derby Stakes at Epsom. A flashy looking chestnut whose breeding was Canadian on both sides, he brought off that rare triple of racing: the Derby Stakes, the Irish

Sweeps Derby at the Curragh and the King George VI and Queen Elizabeth Diamond Stakes at Ascot.

Seattle Slew was American racing's tenth Triple Crown winner. The dark bay son of *Bold Reasoning* was sold for the bargain sum of $17,500, showed amazing speed at two, captured the Crown at three and carried high weights to victory at four. In all three exciting seasons he always showed why he was a champion.

Affirmed was the eleventh Triple Crown winner, the third of the seventies. It was difficult to follow the sensational series of *Secretariat* and *Seattle Slew* and earn the place of prominence that such a feat deserved. But *Affirmed* managed and then some. The chestnut son of *Exclusive Native* had to struggle like no champion before him in order to win. His Triple Crown battles with Calumet Farm's *Alydar* made him one of the most respected horses in American racing. In three memorable seasons he won twenty-two races and a world-record sum of $2,393,818.

Alleged, the bay son of *Hoist the Flag,* was so ignored at the Curragh that he paid off at 33–1, probably the biggest overlay of the decade. At England's York he won the Great Voltigeur Stakes by seven lengths, defeating some of the very three-year-olds his illustrious stablemate *The Minstrel* had struggled with. An incredible horse, *Alleged* won nine of his ten starts and won the rich Prix de l'Arc de Triomphe twice, a feat not accomplished in over twenty years.

Troy, a good looking son of *Petingo,* won the 200th Derby Stakes by seven lengths, the biggest margin since 1925. From the first Wednesday of June at Epsom to the first Sunday of October at Longchamp, *Troy* was undefeated and the rage of British racing. When *Three Troikas* and *Le Marmot* beat him in the Prix de l'Arc de Triomphe, it caused a reaction in British racing circles not seen since *Nijinsky II* 's similar defeat in 1970.

Spectacular Bid, the grey colt by *Bold Bidder,* proved to be one of the most aptly named horses in 1979 racing. He cost only $37,000 as a yearling and ended up being syndicated for a world-record price of $22,000,000. His only mistake was to step on a safety-pin and injure his foot, a freak accident that likely cost him American racing's twelfth Triple Crown. Still racing in 1980, there is a strong chance that he will attain the glory he so richly deserved the year before.

Northern Dancer, the little bay son of *Nearctic,* is Canada's most famous and beloved horse. He was the first and only Canadian-bred to ever win the Kentucky Derby. As a sire he has outdone himself, and it is for this reason that he is a champion of the seventies. He is the only sire of the decade to have two of his offspring win the Epsom Derby. A fascinating horse at the races, he has sired more than five dozen stakes winners, and his name has become synonymous with excellence. He may yet be proclaimed a Sire of the Century.

Some of these horses won with speed to spare, inspiring amazement, disbelief. Some won under the most desperate of circumstances, inspiring a sense of relief and awe. But they all beat the best in difficult tests, and for that they will be long remembered.

In no previous decade has such an impressive collection of champions appeared. Perhaps, as Vanderbilt said, such a thing "just happens". And it may "just happen" again in the eighties, and even again in the nineties. The odds are that it will go on happening so long as people love racing and love even more the horse in racing, the thoroughbred.

The Prix de l'Arc de Triomphe, 1979

On the first Sunday in October, the Prix de l'Arc de Triomphe is run. It is the grand finale to the French racing season and the richest horse race in Europe. It has seen many great champions. *Mill Reef*, *Allez France* and *Alleged* had their victories here in the seventies; *Youth*, *Troy* and *Nijinsky II* failed in the attempt.

Early on this magnificent day, the cool forests and yards of Chantilly echo to the sounds of the great and near-great. Then, with pomp and pageantry, the Republican Guard leads the crowds to Longchamp. Anticipation fills the stands, while intensity is etched upon the faces of jockeys like Lester Piggot on *Trillion*. In 1979, the unexpected happened. The filly *Three Troika's* flew through the stretch to win the great race.

A Portfolio
of Races,
Records and
Bloodlines

Affirmed

Steve Cauthen salutes *Affirmed's* Triple Crown after crossing the finish line in the 1978 Belmont Stakes

Foaled in 1975 in Florida, U.S.A.

COLOUR: *Chestnut*

BRED BY: *Harbor View Farm*

OWNED BY: *Harbor View Farm*

RACING COLOURS:
*Flamingo, white bars on
black sleeve, black cap*

TRAINED BY: *Lazaro S. Barrera*

TOTAL EARNINGS: $2,393,818

PERFORMANCE RECORD:

YEAR	AGE	STARTS	FIRSTS	SECONDS	THIRDS
1977	2	9	7	2	0
1978	3	11	8	2	0
1979	4	9	7	1	1
TOTALS		29	22	5	1

AFFIRMED
Chestnut colt
1975

- *Exclusive Native*
  - *Raise a Native*
    - *Native Dancer*
      - *Polynesian*
      - *Geisha*
    - *Raise You*
      - *Case Ace*
      - *Lady Glory*
  - *Exclusive*
    - *Shut Out*
      - *Equipoise*
      - *Goose Egg*
    - *Good Example*
      - *Pilate*
      - *Parade Girl*
- *Won't Tell You*
  - *Crafty Admiral*
    - *Fighting Fox*
      - *Sir Gallahad* III
      - *Marguerite*
    - *Admiral's Lady*
      - *War Admiral*
      - *Boola Brook*
  - *Scarlet Ribbon*
    - *Volcanic*
      - *Ambrose Light*
      - *Hot Supper*
    - *Native Valor*
      - *Mahmoud*
      - *Native Gal*

Alleged

Lester Piggott rides *Alleged* to the bay's second triumph in the Prix de l'Arc de Triomphe (1978)

Foaled in 1975 in Kentucky, U.S.A.

COLOUR: *Bay*

BRED BY: *Mrs. June McKnight*

OWNED BY: *Robert Sangster*

RACING COLOURS:
Green and white ball sash,
blue sleeves, green dots
on white cap

TRAINED BY: *Vincent O'Brien*

TOTAL EARNINGS: £327,315

PERFORMANCE RECORD:

YEAR	AGE	STARTS	FIRSTS	SECONDS	THIRDS
1976	2	1	1	0	0
1977	3	6	5	1	0
1978	4	3	3	0	0
TOTALS		10	9	1	0

ALLEGED
Bay colt
1975

- Hoist the Flag
  - Tom Rolfe
    - Ribot
      - Tenerani
      - Romanella
    - Pocahontas
      - Roman
      - How
  - Wavy Navy
    - War Admiral
      - Man o'War
      - Brushup
    - Triomphe
      - Tourbillon
      - Melibee
- Princess Pout
  - Prince John
    - Princequillo
      - Prince Rose
      - Cosquilla
    - Not Afraid
      - Count Fleet
      - Banish Fear
  - Determined Lady
    - Determine
      - Alibhai
      - Koubis
    - Tumbling
      - War Admiral
      - Up The Hill

Allez France

Allez France, with Yves Saint-Martin up, battles *Comtesse de Loir* to win the 1974 Prix de l'Arc de Triomphe

Foaled in 1970 in Kentucky, U.S.A.

COLOUR: Bay

BRED BY: Bieber-Jacobs Stable

OWNED BY: Daniel Wildenstein

RACING COLOURS:
Royal blue, light blue epaulets,
light blue cap

TRAINED BY: Angel Penna;
      Albert Klimscha

TOTAL EARNINGS: $1,386,146

PERFORMANCE RECORD:

YEAR	AGE	STARTS	FIRSTS	SECONDS	THIRDS
1972	2	2	2	0	0
1973	3	7	3	2	0
1974	4	5	5	0	0
1975	5	7	3	1	1
TOTALS		21	13	3	1

ALLEZ FRANCE
Bay filly
1970

- Sea-Bird II
  - Dan Cupid
    - Native Dancer
      - Polynesian
      - Geisha
    - Vixenette
      - Sickle
      - Lady Reynard
  - Sicalade
    - Sicambre
      - Prince Bio
      - Sif
    - Marmalade
      - Maurepas
      - Couleur
- Priceless Gem
  - Hail to Reason
    - Turn-to
      - Royal Charger
      - Source Sucree
    - Nothirdchance
      - Blue Swords
      - Galla Colors
  - Searching
    - War Admiral
      - Man o' War
      - Brushup
    - Big Hurry
      - Black Toney
      - La Troienne

163

Dahlia

Dahlia, ridden by Lester Piggott, outruns *Big Spruce* to win the 1974 Canadian International Championship Stakes

Foaled in 1970 in Kentucky, U.S.A.

COLOUR: *Chestnut*

BRED BY: *Nelson Bunker Hunt*

OWNED BY: *Nelson Bunker Hunt*

RACING COLOURS:
Light and dark green blocks,
light green sleeves and cap

TRAINED BY: *Maurice Zilber;*
Charles Whittingham

TOTAL EARNINGS: $1,544,139

PERFORMANCE RECORD:

YEAR	AGE	STARTS	FIRSTS	SECONDS	THIRDS
1972	2	2	0	1	0
1973	3	10	6	1	1
1974	4	10	5	0	3
1975	5	11	1	0	3
1976	6	13	2	0	1
TOTALS		46	14	2	8

DAHLIA
Chestnut filly
1970

- Vaguely Noble
  - Vienna
    - Aureole
      - Hyperion
      - Angelola
    - Turkish Blood
      - Turkhan
      - Rusk
  - Noble Lassie
    - Nearco
      - Pharos
      - Nogara
    - Belle Sauvage
      - Big Game
      - Tropical Sun
- Charming Alibi
  - Honeys Alibi
    - Alibhai
      - Hyperion
      - Teresina
    - Honeymoon
      - Beau Pere
      - Panoramic
  - Adorada II
    - Hierocles
      - Abjer
      - Loika
    - Gilded Wave
      - Gallant Fox
      - Ondulation

Exceller

Bill Shoemaker urges *Exceller* **(far right) on to a close victory over** *Text* **(centre) and** *Vigors* **in the 1978 Hollywood Gold Cup**

Foaled in 1973 in Kentucky, U.S.A.

COLOUR: *Bay*

BRED BY: *Mrs. Charles Engelhard*

OWNED BY: *Belair Stud, Ltd.* and
Nelson Bunker Hunt

RACING COLOURS:
White, green hoops, tie and cap

TRAINED BY: *Francois Mathet;*
Maurice Zilber;
Charles Whittingham

TOTAL EARNINGS: $1,569,002

PERFORMANCE RECORD:

YEAR	AGE	STARTS	FIRSTS	SECONDS	THIRDS
1975	2	4	2	0	1
1976	3	6	4	1	0
1977	4	9	3	2	2
1978	5	10	7	1	0
1979	6	4	0	1	2
TOTALS		33	16	5	5

EXCELLER
Bay colt
1973

- Vaguely Noble
  - Vienna
    - Aureole
      - Hyperion
      - Angelola
    - Turkish Blood
      - Turkhan
      - Rusk
  - Noble Lassie
    - Nearco
      - Pharos
      - Nogara
    - Belle Sauvage
      - Big Game
      - Tropical Sun
- Too Bold
  - Bald Eagle
    - Nasrullah
      - Nearco
      - Mumtaz Begum
    - Siama
      - Tiger
      - China Face
  - Hidden Talent
    - Dark Star
      - Royal Gem II
      - Isolde
    - Dangerous Dame
      - Nasrullah
      - Lady Kells

167

Forego

Forego (No. 2) and Bill Shoemaker come up on the outside for an ultimately victorious run through the stretch in the 1976 Woodward Stakes

Foaled in 1970 in Kentucky, U.S.A.

COLOUR: *Bay*

BRED BY: *Lazy F Ranch*

OWNED BY: *Lazy F Ranch*

RACING COLOURS:
*Yellow, black sleeves and hoop,
yellow cap*

TRAINED BY: *Sherril W. Ward;
Frank Y. Whiteley Jr.*

TOTAL EARNINGS: $1,938,957

PERFORMANCE RECORD:

YEAR	AGE	STARTS	FIRSTS	SECONDS	THIRDS
1973	3	18	9	3	3
1974	4	13	8	2	2
1975	5	9	6	1	1
1976	6	8	6	1	1
1977	7	7	4	2	0
1978	8	2	1	0	0
TOTALS		57	34	9	7

FOREGO
Bay gelding
1970

- Forli
  - Aristophanes
    - Hyperion
      - Gainsborough
      - Selene
    - Commotion
      - Mieuxce
      - Riot
  - Trevisa
    - Advocate
      - Fair Trial
      - Guiding Star
    - Veneta
      - Foxglove
      - Dogaresa
- Lady Golconda
  - Hasty Road
    - Roman
      - Sir Gallahad III
      - Buckup
    - Traffic Court
      - Discovery
      - Traffic
  - Girlea
    - Bull Lea
      - Bull Dog
      - Rose Leaves
    - Whirling Girl
      - Whirlaway
      - Nellie Flag

Grundy

Grundy, ridden by Pat Eddery, decisively wins the 1975 Derby Stakes at Epsom

Foaled in 1972 in Gloucestershire, England

COLOUR: *Chestnut*

BRED BY: *Overbury Stud*

OWNED BY: *Dr. Carlo Vittadini*

RACING COLOURS:
Dark blue, yellow hoop,
sleeves and spots on cap

TRAINED BY: *Peter Walwyn*

TOTAL EARNINGS: £326,421

PERFORMANCE RECORD:

YEAR	AGE	STARTS	FIRSTS	SECONDS	THIRDS
1974	2	4	4	0	0
1975	3	7	4	2	0
TOTALS		11	8	2	0

GRUNDY
Chestnut colt
1972

- Great Nephew
  - Honeyway
    - Fairway
      - Phalaris
      - Scapa Flow
    - Honey Buzzard
      - Papyrus
      - Lady Peregrine
  - Sybil's Niece
    - Admiral's Walk
      - Hyperion
      - Tabaris
    - Sybil's Sister
      - Nearco
      - Sister Sarah
- Word From Lundy
  - Worden II
    - Wild Risk
      - Rialto
      - Wild Violet
    - Sans Tares
      - Sind
      - Tara
  - Lundy Princess
    - Princely Gift
      - Nasrullah
      - Blue Gem
    - Lundy Parrot
      - Flamingo
      - Waterval

Mill Reef

Mill Reef (foreground), ridden by Geoff Lewis, wins the 1971 King George VI and Queen Elizabeth Stakes at Ascot

Foaled in 1968 in Virginia, U.S.A.

COLOUR: *Bay*

BRED BY: *Paul Mellon*

OWNED BY: *Paul Mellon*

RACING COLOURS:
*Black, gold cross and
stripe on cap*

TRAINED BY: *Ian Balding*

TOTAL EARNINGS: £301,218

PERFORMANCE RECORD:

YEAR	AGE	STARTS	FIRSTS	SECONDS	THIRDS
1970	2	6	5	1	0
1971	3	6	5	1	0
1972	4	2	2	0	0
TOTALS		14	12	2	0

MILL REEF
Bay colt
1968

Never Bend
— Nasrullah
— — Nearco
— — — Pharos
— — — Nogara
— — Mumtaz Begum
— — — Blenheim
— — — Mumtaz Mahal
— Lalun
— — Djeddah
— — — Djebel
— — — Djezima
— — Be Faithful
— — — Bimelech
— — — Bloodroot

Milan Mill
— Princequillo
— — Prince Rose
— — — Rose Prince
— — — Indolence
— — Cosquilla
— — — Papyrus
— — — Quick Thought
— Virginia Water
— — Count Fleet
— — — Reigh Count
— — — Quickly
— — Red Ray
— — — Hyperion
— — — Infra Red

The Minstrel

The Minstrel (white blaze), ridden by Lester Piggott, emerges victorious from
a desperate battle with *Orange Bay* to win the 1977 King George VI and
Queen Elizabeth Diamond Stakes at Ascot, while *Exceller* rushes to a third-place finish

Foaled in 1974 in Ontario, Canada

COLOUR: *Chestnut*

BRED BY: *E.P. Taylor*

OWNED BY: *Robert Sangster*

RACING COLOURS:
*Green and white ball sash, blue
sleeves, green dots on white cap*

TRAINED BY: *Vincent O'Brien*

TOTAL EARNINGS: **$570,748**

PERFORMANCE RECORD:

YEAR	AGE	STARTS	FIRSTS	SECONDS	THIRDS
1976	2	3	3	0	0
1977	3	6	4	1	1
TOTALS		9	7	1	1

THE MINSTREL
Chestnut colt
1974

- Northern Dancer
  - Nearctic
    - Nearco
      - Pharos
      - Nogara
    - Lady Angela
      - Hyperion
      - Sister Sarah
  - Natalma
    - Native Dancer
      - Polynesian
      - Geisha
    - Almahmoud
      - Mahmoud
      - Arbitrator
- Fleur
  - Victoria Park
    - Chop Chop
      - Flares
      - Sceptical
    - Victoriana
      - Windfields
      - Iribelle
  - Flaming Page
    - Bull Page
      - Bull Lea
      - Our Page
    - Flaring Top
      - Menow
      - Flaming Top

Nijinsky II

Nijinsky II and Lester Piggott (between the two horses wearing nose-bands) round Tattenham Corner in the 1970 Epsom Derby

Foaled in 1967 in Ontario, Canada

COLOUR: *Bay*

BRED BY: *E.P. Taylor*

OWNED BY: *Charles Engelhard*

RACING COLOURS:
*Green, scarlet sash,
yellow sleeves, green cap*

TRAINED BY: *Vincent O'Brien*

TOTAL EARNINGS: $677,163

PERFORMANCE RECORD:

YEAR	AGE	STARTS	FIRSTS	SECONDS	THIRDS
1969	2	5	5	0	0
1970	3	8	6	2	0
TOTALS		13	11	2	0

NIJINSKY II
Bay colt
1967

- Northern Dancer
  - Nearctic
    - Nearco
      - Pharos
      - Nogara
    - Lady Angela
      - Hyperion
      - Sister Sarah
  - Natalma
    - Native Dancer
      - Polynesian
      - Geisha
    - Almahmoud
      - Mahmoud
      - Arbitrator
- Flaming Page
  - Bull Page
    - Bull Lea
      - Bull Dog
      - Rose Leaves
    - Our Page
      - Blue Larkspur
      - Occult
  - Flaring Top
    - Menow
      - Pharamond
      - Alcibiades
    - Flaming Top
      - Omaha
      - Firetop

Northern Dancer

Northern Dancer, Bill Hartack up, holds *Hill Rise* even to win the 1964 Kentucky Derby

Foaled in 1961 in Ontario, Canada

COLOUR: *Bay*

BRED BY: *E. P. Taylor*

OWNED BY: *Windfields Farm*

RACING COLOURS:
Turquoise, gold cap and spots on sleeve

TRAINED BY: *Horatio Luro*

TOTAL EARNINGS: $580,806

PERFORMANCE RECORD:

YEAR	AGE	STARTS	FIRSTS	SECONDS	THIRDS
1963	2	9	7	2	0
1964	3	9	7	0	2
TOTALS		18	14	2	2

NORTHERN DANCER
Bay colt
1961

- Nearctic
  - Nearco
    - Pharos
      - Phalaris
      - Scapa Flow
    - Nogara
      - Havresac II
      - Catnip
  - Lady Angela
    - Hyperion
      - Gainsborough
      - Selene
    - Sister Sarah
      - Abbots Trace
      - Sarita
- Natalma
  - Native Dancer
    - Polynesian
      - Unbreakable
      - Black Polly
    - Geisha
      - Discovery
      - Miyako
  - Almahmoud
    - Mahmoud
      - Blenheim II
      - Mah Mahal
    - Arbitrator
      - Peace Chance
      - Mother Goose

Red Rum

Red Rum, ridden by Brian Fletcher, jumps the last fence to win the Grand National at Aintree for the first time (1973)

Foaled in 1965 in County Meath, Ireland

PERFORMANCE RECORD:

COLOUR: *Bay*

BRED BY: *Martin McEnery*

OWNED BY: *Noel Le Mare*

RACING COLOURS:
*Maroon, yellow diamond
on body and cap*

TRAINED BY: *Donald McCain*

TOTAL EARNINGS: £146,409.80

YEAR	AGE	STARTS	FIRSTS	SECONDS	THIRDS
1967	2	8	2	0	2*
1968	3	2	1	1	0*
1968-69	3	10	3	2	2‡
1969-70	4	14	0	2	1‡
1970-71	5	13	3	0	7‡
1971-72	6	12	2	1	3‡
1972-73	7	9	6	1	1‡
1973-74	8	10	6	3	0‡
1974-75	9	8	2	2	1‡
1975-76	10	10	0	1	3‡
1976-77	11	9	2	0	3‡
1977-78	12	5	0	2	0‡
TOTALS		110	27	15	23

RED RUM
*Bay gelding
1965*

- Quorum
  - Vilmorin
    - Gold Bridge
      - Swynford
      - Flying Diadem
    - Queen of the Meadows
      - Fairway
      - Queen of the Blues
  - Akimbo
    - Bois Roussel
      - Vatout
      - Plucky Liege
    - Bulolo
      - Noble Star
      - Pussy Willow
- Mared
  - Magic Red
    - Link Boy
      - Pharos
      - Market Girl
    - Infra Red
      - Ethnarch
      - Black Ray
  - Quinta
    - Anwar
      - Umidwar
      - Stafaralla
    - Batika
      - Blenheim
      - Brise Bise

*Flat / ‡Under the rules of racing over obstacles

Seattle Slew

Seattle Slew and Jean Cruguet take the first jewel in the Triple Crown, the 1977 Kentucky Derby

Foaled in 1974 in Kentucky, *U.S.A.*

COLOUR: *Dark bay or brown*

BRED BY: *Ben S. Castleman*

OWNED BY: *Tayhill Stable*

RACING COLOURS:
Black jacket with yellow yoke,
black and yellow sleeves,
with multiple hoops,
yellow cap with black pompom

TRAINED BY: *William Turner Jr.;*
Douglas Peterson

TOTAL EARNINGS: $1,208,726

PERFORMANCE RECORD:

YEAR	AGE	STARTS	FIRSTS	SECONDS	THIRDS
1976	2	3	3	0	0
1977	3	7	6	0	0
1978	4	7	5	2	0
TOTALS		17	14	2	0

SEATTLE SLEW
Dark bay or brown colt
1974

- Bold Reasoning
  - Bolnesian
    - Bold Ruler
      - Nasrullah
      - Miss Disco
    - Alanesian
      - Polynesian
      - Alablue
  - Reason to Earn
    - Hail to Reason
      - Turn-to
      - Nothirdchance
    - Sailing Home
      - Wait a Bit
      - Marching Home
- My Charmer
  - Poker
    - Round Table
      - Princequillo
      - Knight's Daughter
    - Glamour
      - Nasrullah
      - Striking
  - Fair Charmer
    - Jet Action
      - Jet Pilot
      - Busher
    - Myrtle Charm
      - Alsab
      - Crepe Myrtle

Secretariat

Ron Turcotte looks back in disbelief as *Secretariat* becomes the first Triple Crown winner in twenty-five years with his devastating thirty-one-length victory in the 1973 Belmont Stakes

Foaled in 1970 in Virginia, U.S.A.

COLOUR: *Chestnut*

BRED BY: *Meadow Stud*

OWNED BY: *Meadow Stable*

RACING COLOURS:
*Blue and white blocks, blue sleeves,
white stripes, blue cap*

TRAINED BY: *Lucien Laurin*

TOTAL EARNINGS: $1,316,808

PERFORMANCE RECORD:

YEAR	AGE	STARTS	FIRSTS	SECONDS	THIRDS
1972	2	9	7	1	0
1973	3	12	9	2	1
TOTALS		21	16	3	1

SECRETARIAT
Chestnut colt
1970

- Bold Ruler
  - Nasrullah
    - Nearco
      - Pharos
      - Nogara
    - Mumtaz Begum
      - Blenheim II
      - Mumtaz Mahal
  - Miss Disco
    - Discovery
      - Display
      - Ariadne
    - Outdone
      - Pompey
      - Sweep Out
- Somethingroyal
  - Princequillo
    - Prince Rose
      - Rose Prince
      - Indolence
    - Cosquilla
      - Papyrus
      - Quick Thought
  - Imperatrice
    - Caruso
      - Polymelian
      - Sweet Music
    - Cinquepace
      - Brown Bud
      - Assignation

185

Spectacular Bid

Spectacular Bid, ridden by Bill Shoemaker, wins the 1979 Marlboro Cup

Foaled in 1976 in Kentucky, U.S.A.

COLOUR: *Grey*

BRED BY: *Mrs. W. Gilmore* and *Mrs. W. Jason*

OWNED BY: *Hawksworth Farm*

RACING COLOURS:
*Blue, black cross sashes,
blue bars on black sleeves, black cap*

TRAINED BY: *Grover Delp*

TOTAL EARNINGS: $1,663,817

PERFORMANCE RECORD:

YEAR	AGE	STARTS	FIRSTS	SECONDS	THIRDS
1978	2	9	7	1	0
1979	3	12	10	1	1
TOTALS		21	17	2	1

SPECTACULAR BID
Grey colt
1976

- Bold Bidder
  - Bold Ruler
    - Nasrullah
      - Nearco
      - Mumtaz Begum
    - Miss Disco
      - Discovery
      - Outdone
  - High Bid
    - To Market
      - Market Wise
      - Pretty Does
    - Stepping Stone
      - Princequillo
      - Step Across
- Spectacular
  - Promised Land
    - Palestinian
      - Sun Again
      - Dolly Whisk
    - Mahmoudess
      - Mahmoud
      - Forever Yours
  - Stop on Red
    - To Market
      - Market Wise
      - Pretty Does
    - Danger Ahead
      - Head Play
      - Lady Beware

Troy

Troy, with Willie Carson up, wins the 200th Derby Stakes by an awesome seven-length margin

Foaled in 1976 in County Meath, Ireland

COLOUR: *Bay*

BRED BY: *Ballymacoll Stud Farm Ltd.*

OWNED BY: *Sir Michael Sobell*

RACING COLOURS:
Pale blue, yellow and white check cap

TRAINED BY: *W.R. Hern*

TOTAL EARNINGS: £450,494

PERFORMANCE RECORD:

YEAR	AGE	STARTS	FIRSTS	SECONDS	THIRDS
1978	2	4	2	2	0
1979	3	7	6	0	1
TOTALS		11	8	2	1

TROY
Bay colt
1976

- Petingo
  - Petition
    - Fair Trial
      - Fairway
      - Lady Juror
    - Art Paper
      - Artist's Proof
      - Quire
  - Alcazar
    - Alycidon
      - Donatello II
      - Aurora
    - Quarterdeck
      - Nearco
      - Poker Chip
- La Milo
  - Hornbeam
    - Hyperion
      - Gainsborough
      - Selene
    - Thicket
      - Nasrullah
      - Thorn Wood
  - Pin Prick
    - Pinza
      - Chanteur II
      - Pasqua
    - Miss Winston
      - Royal Charger
      - East Wantleye

Youth

Youth and Sandy Hawley gallop to an easy victory in the
1976 Canadian International Championship Stakes at Toronto's Woodbine

Foaled in 1973 in Maryland, U.S.A.

COLOUR: *Bay*

BRED BY: *Nelson Bunker Hunt*

OWNED BY: *Nelson Bunker Hunt*

RACING COLOURS:
Light and dark green blocks,
light green sleeves and cap

TRAINED BY: *Maurice Zilber*

TOTAL EARNINGS: $683,224

PERFORMANCE RECORD:

YEAR	AGE	STARTS	FIRSTS	SECONDS	THIRDS
1975	2	2	1	1	0
1976	3	9	7	0	1
TOTALS		11	8	1	1

YOUTH
Bay colt
1973

- Ack Ack
  - Battle Joined
    - Armageddon
      - Alsab
      - Fighting Lady
    - Ethel Walker
      - Revoked
      - Ethel Terry
  - Fast Turn
    - Turn-to
      - Royal Charger
      - Source Sucree
    - Cherokee Rose
      - Princequillo
      - The Squaw II
- Gazala II
  - Dark Star
    - Royal Gem II
      - Dhoti
      - French Gem
    - Isolde
      - Bull Dog
      - Fiji
  - Belle Angevine
    - L'Amiral
      - Admiral Drake
      - Hurrylor
    - Bella II
      - Canot
      - Bayan Kara

Black and white photographs
appear with the permission of:

P. Bertrand et fils, pp. 160, 162;
Michael Burns, pp. 164, 190;
Bob Coglianese, pp. 158, 168, 184, 186;
Hollywood Park, p. 166;
PAPL, pp. 170, 172, 176, 188;
Churchill Downs, Inc., pp. 178, 182;
Alec Russell, pp. 174, 180.

2